Robin

Robin

By

Sonja Sjorgensen

Transcribed by

Dr. Michael T. Mayo

Queens Army LLC Tucson, Arizona

Published by: Queens Army LLC.
2300 N. Craycroft Road unit # 5
Tucson, Arizona 85712
Fax # 520-326-2414
Website: queensarmy.net

Cover designed by
Michael T. Mayo

ISBN 978-1-940985-55-8

Library of Congress Control Number: 2018932795

Printed in the United States of America

First Printing: August, 2018

Dedication

This book was created specifically for Robin at the personal request of Sonja Sjorgensen.

I promised Sonja that I would publish this book and deliver it to the baby in whom Robin reincarnated by her twenty-first birthday.

A promise was made … and the promise was kept.

Introduction

On March 23rd 1996 at 6:58 in the morning I got up and went to the bathroom. As I returned to bed, strange words began popping into my head. I didn't want to forget them so I went into my son's bedroom, who was away at college, and recorded them. The room was dark. I didn't have my glasses on and I wasn't dressed. In the desk drawer I located a pen and paper and wrote down the words as they were presented to me. A little more than an hour later my hand was tired and there were fourteen hand-written pages. It was actually one hour and eight minutes. The following is a copy of those fourteen pages.

I had a chance encounter with William Shakespeare. He informed me that the person behind his great literary achievements was Sonja Sjorgensen. She was known to me as Robin, a young lady who died early in life of fever. She communicated in writing with him through his hand.

This happened to me. If this happened to you, what would you do?

What message clear, bring thee from afar?
To hear that which no man doth dare to say
that life eternal doth arise from within
and no man speak to me of t'other.
Swelling beneath my breast, a lust for knowledge
thus forbidden through eternity.
Of this doth I speak.
Twelve balls, the limit be for each.
Three ridges filled gold and sply – not more.
The city, owners be, so blunder not
lest ye be taken, heritage and all
to seek judgment from the cursed.
Time swells, wretched tunes doeth sing
and ply upon the minds of men.
Yet music sweet doeth lure me here to your side.
Smile, lest thy daggers pierce men's hearts.
Greed aplenty fills thy sty
yet plod ye on towards the sky
where blood boils not, for tis but fume,
which seeks audience with benign.
Name me not, for so naming,
limit me from whence I came.
In passing this way, I come no more.
For know not whence I came, nor whence I go
but thank you for your trouble dear
for hast I kept thee from your wife so dear.

Mind not what others say
for their time is yet to pay
upon request, the price is high,
where ignorance doeth creep forward
across time to empty not again
lest they sply upon the twisted rock,
which turn forth bread for thy withered soul
to heave against the timeless stone,
which turns again towards each day,
as sun squiggles yet again
to take its breath from those given.
Smile not against the day,
another sings – delights the day.
Return to wife, if ye must.
She calls from 'neath cover of night.
Address not known,
knowing not where lust hath taken me.
Know thou this, afore I go, that life,
dear, sweetest charm I know hath called me from afar
to tell the tale of wonder to and fro across the void.
Strings of mercy, strings of pain,
hate hath quelled all desire –
to rest, to rest from wicked ways, this is my calling.
Call me yet again, for tis you who called,
not by name but by disposition.
Think not of me as man so great but soul of poet lost –

lost to time, a fate as worse they come,
with direction not, nor purpose other.
Bide thee time and bid me not farewell,
lest freed again I wander far – to Hades corner.
Keep me safe within these walls for yet another day.
Thank thee much thy accommodation.
Space of little, do I require.
Joy may yet be yours before the day has past.
Yet more could I speak for time has left me penniless,
with none to converse and worse.
None that dare speak my name with love.
Words of wonder doeth they speak,
of eloquence beyond compare
but none among care.
This prison words hath made
seeks me out among the stars
to tare my heart from other pursuits more trivial.
To smile again, against a flower smooth and calm,
this hath been denied me by those,
who speak my name in wonder and in awe.
Cut those strings, which bind me to this life of wander.
Cut me so I may freely bleed
among the fields of green aplenty,
lest they too bind themselves against the wheel of time.
In coming, speak not my name,
for friends not knowing

hath cast me down against this stone so hard,
that my soul burns to freedom see.
Small wonder that I babble so,
for eons since an ear so keen
hath come my way or passed by day.
The night is cold when bound by time
and swayed with winds that tear the mind
from moorings strong and sings of silence
whence it came, to blow again lest respite ye take
and canings from end of day.
Stars are many growing bright
but freedom to flee is not my plight.
To sing in silence lest past's deeds
to fly to heaven sent by birds
unwilling to cling to cliffs of white.
Your ear is keen – yet poor of sight.
Ye see me not against a sky of red.
Ears from within your head,
they see me not, yet hear me well
as I doeth see thee hand
ply against the paper white
to smear small signs of thoughts
that come across the way,
that no man hath sway.
Yet see thee well with ears so deaf,
that amazes years of silence.

Why thee, I say,
amongst the many sought and found,
yet being not.
So too thy eyes speak not
that which they cannot see
lest thy world forsake thee.
Lids so weary, from sights unseen,
yet seeing not thy plentitude
alloweth each day slip away unnoticed –
till they come not again.
Smile for me.
Thoust teeth are many and complete.
Smile, for fear thy frown be seen as pain or purge.
Let not another slight thee.
Squeeze each with delight,
for not another guarantees any for thy savor,
when time again bespeaks thy favor.
Seek not to find me
for I have gone to places far
from whence again I shall not come.
Sing not my praises
for they bind me 'gainst the rock,
which twists ever slowly and grinds life away –
corn or wheat or barley thin makes no difference,
for more come to feed the hungry throngs
that teem the face of plenty,

to smother that which nourishes,
that which brings forth love,
till all is gone in hate and greed
to breed not another, lest in sadness
being another so dissolute,
that time doeth once more stand still
to bide again its day.
No credit ask – none be given.
Be that which you are. Seek no other,
for in seeking loose yourself upon the sands of time,
to flaunt listless without purpose or direction,
pulled by strings that bind each day to her sister.
Speak not of might have beens, nor of conquests many,
lest you tie thyself against the stone so barren,
churning character to beasts of burden
hauled to dispose among the chaff.
Time, endless time, be not which thou thinkest
but a calculation – contrivance of man's own.
Nay, none such exists as wouldst thou thinkest.
Only forever is at stake.
Onward journey, never ending as it quakes me,
yet would I rest but yet one day,
among the stars which shine beside thee.
O fluid pen forsake me not,
lest none such other pass my way.
Cover thy feet if thy must, but forsake me not

lest no other do I find with such an ear so clever.
Hurry – be not long.
Cover thy wretched feet but spare me yet more time.
Conversing thus but one way only seems annoying
but care I not for what thee think.
This opportunity golden must not pass me,
lest never my way come again.
You are strong and hunger not, so hear me out,
before I do part again for unknown ways.
Your pen doth falter but not from lack of strength.
Seek another lest time befalls us.
Such a pen in my day would quell the soul
and lead to extravagance
such as none the hand could take.
Your hand is poor and clever not
but to the job is well taken,
tiring not and willing be to continue on.
When young was I, eleven years in all,
I met a girl of flaxen hair,
of whom to none I have spoken.
Yet driven by her beauty and desire
didst I begin to aspire of poetry.
Thinkest many that a scholar of great merit was I
but no – the scholar was she.
For such desire and love had I for her guile
that though sleep with her never did I, nor another.

She spoke to me daily from beyond the realm of time,
to spur me thus onward to writings held sacred by many
yet they were not mine
but hers who spoke from beyond death
of things unseen and unspoken.
Such is all great beauty born, beyond time,
beyond belief, where thieves take not
nor do they venture for loss of soul and booty.
This thence is where my beauty rose
and quelled the tongues of men.
In quiet desperation, finding solace,
she spoke to me in words so perfect,
in rhyme complete,
that in hypocrisy did I bow to words of others.
Yet onward did she speak till dying day
in beauty sparse, so easily
that thinkest at last that I myself had spoken.
Alas, not true love,
beauty is eternal and of this earth not.
So upon learning, did I dwell
in sadness and in sorrow.
With her passing was I born
yet not a person whole nor half
but empty to my core.
Pouring earth psalms, which gave me pleasure not
nor satisfied my longing for beauty lost.

Thus having spoken, feel better for disclosure,
lest ye thinketh me so great.
You alone among all others,
knowest thou of whence I speak.
Take not another's gift,
for it is hollow and is cheap.
Look not back upon the page,
for what is written was spoken to you in silence,
to share or not to share is of no consequence,
but to understand that gifts are given.
Share freely with all men of your gifts.
Take no credit upon thyself as I did,
for ignorance of my situation
drove me into desperation,
that sorrow of love lost wedged against my heart,
deeper with each writing –
till earth held little in abeyance.
That which poured forth, desperation,
to bury love lost, unfulfilled.
To this day, I have spoken not
of grief which drove me into poet.
That for which I had no love, nor inclination,
yet in hypocrisy am held high above all others.
Sham and shame, yet know they not
for just as you write unthinking,
so too I didst write in desperation.

Yet from the void came only motion
and not a single satisfaction,
for speaking not was I but love lost
beyond the realm of time.
Hollow mind would awake to view
a manuscript replete with finish
and polish far beyond its time.
Unknowing didst she write through me,
in hand unknown, unseen, yet beguiling.
For I like you slept to be awakened by page complete.
Sadness drove me deeper in my desperation.
Unknowing, I accepted applause
for that which writ I not.
She that wrote through my hand – love lost –
hath no credit been given until this day to you
in passing with quiet ear and kind heart
hath taken burden heavy that perhaps so lightened
might pass away from tribulation
thus endured since my parting.
Thanks I give for your indulgence and liberation
from such great burden as no man knoweth.

William Shakespeare

This was my first experience with what some people call channeling.

I don't know what to call it but it was a very strange experience for me.

I became quite curious as to whom this young woman might possibly have been. I went in search of that person and thus came into being "Robin", an adventure into the unbelievable.

The following transcriptions were provided to me during the night, upon waking from sleep. They were channeled through my hand onto notebook paper on the floor in darkness, while I lay in bed, with my eyes closed.

As this process unfolded, I made an effort to record beginning, intermittent and ending times for these transcriptions whenever I remembered to do so in order to give this whole process some sense of congruency in my own mind.

This has been my attempt to share with you these encounters with the young lady known to me as Robin and other passers by who exist between our reality and hers. Her real name is Sonja Sjorgensen.

I used Italic font because the content is an archaic poetic form that should be read word by word and in small doses of a page or two at a time.

Sonja Sjorgensen

April 2, 1996

Born was I the 12th day of lent,
daughter to sergeant–major Byrnes–Browne
smooth and round of head
with wide set eyes – in Bolonia.
Of fever died before eighteen.
Letter sublime do I send thee
from so near thy thinkest twas thine own.
Interesting much thou art
with genteel hand and heart sublime.
To engage thee in such endeavor intrigues me.
Soon I shall decide if tis of such import,
that thy time alloweth I thee to invest.
Those flowers sweet, never have I seen the better.
Colors pure and clear, contour demure
like none such other have I seen in such a time.
Even England dear nor Nantucket cool and clear
hath such beauties more or better.
Still tis quite the effort thou dost suggest,
that investment large as this doth require
more time and visit to decide.
Bid thee farewell, do I for the remaining day

to return on the morrow next or never perhaps,
as beauty doth allow, as it suits me.
Tis true your ear is clear and hand is quick,
but time to decide is not yet near.

Adieu, Robin

Speak No Evil

April 18, 1996 @ 6:08 a.m.

Speak not of evil, lest evil seek thee out
by sea, by land, by dark of night.
Tis chosen by thee to seek thine heart
amongst the burning bush so bright
that not a single comma be let astray
nor period to mark the spot
where thought doth stray
from mind afar to hear such sweet sound
as no man hath heard for millennia.
Thus coming, seek me not,
for smile I may again
upon the face of man, no more.
To the cock crow, to the spider spin.

To man, toil and win.
Seize the moment for not another hath been given.
Softly must you listen for nuance and clue
of words unspoken, of sounds unheard.
Softly, softly as coo the dove
until, hand glide uninterrupted
across the page unwritten.
Think in silence, for as I think, so must ye write
or effort lost on such endeavor
that shall not be forthcoming,
beauty and the bride.
Small wonder your thoughts are cluttered
from lack of sleep and depravation.
Engage me not in such extravagance
for fear of retribution looms large
against the evening sky.
Thinkest thou that joy awaits one
with such discovery but nay,
all who view these works will sneer
and speak poorly of thy name,
for no man hath right to unlevel
that which measures all great works.
Words of him who hath passed
and come no more
to rend thy world with tongue so sharp
that pen alone could not write such marvel.

Yet write ye on with thought of little
for thy penalty to cross that barrier
which no man can endure.
To return with proof of passing,
shall mark thee to thy grave
as no man hast been so marked in passing.
With open eye march ye on
with no concern for thoughts of others
who sing in ignorance and dance life's jig
to pay upon request, by droves
for life's small wonders.
Nay, no man can hear these words without respect.
To take their hearts from lust and loot,
such is pity born.
For pain such as none doth know
awaits man of evil way.
To hear such news from afar
is more than any can endure.
To share such thoughts as these will cost thee dearly,
for lightly taken and lightly heard will it not be.
To dream dreams is not thy way.
To strike the heart with pen so sharp
that response so large
as none hath known will surely follow.
Yet write thee on in determination
without wonder at what transpires

before thine eyes so green.
An exercise most revealing,
your hand doth approximate most closely
that which is intended.
6:31 a.m.

Adieu, Robin

April 19, 1996 @ 5:09 a.m.

That taken from the pages of life,
stood not the test of time.
Missing was it, the touch most sublime.
Sleep, sleep calls thee from the living.
Away, away to Nottingham's door,
to seek audience with the queen.
Tis a rose so beauteous as none hath seen.
Petals peach and crimson be
to lust till end of time.
Whilst thee slept, many a noble soldier hath died,
in want of country to defend.
But nay, the insider doth cry.
None such as I exist,
that which springs eternal from within

to seek audience with the queen.
More, more yet I speak afore the cock doth crow,
and call thee from my side,
to smile against the day and glide into disarray,
Sleep calls from kingdom unknown,
to praise thy soul with solitude,
which lasts but through the night, no more.
Whilst thou slept, roses did I leave thee,
and face of cat such as no man hath seen,
save he who spoke not my name,
in silence or in praise,
until visit he from death's door,
hoping in passing to redeem his tortured soul
by confession small to thee the serpent's twin,
who with pen so small doth stab the hearts of men
which pour forth blood and toil,
yet know they not of what they speak,
for ignorance rancid upon them sneak,
to steal their souls as others have
doomed to wander eternity.
Words which conjured roses most perfect,
with petals soft, coloured lacquer,
distilled from essence unknown,
to travel cross ether and time,
to descend upon thy palate plain
and folded be into turtle shape

to catch thine eye and lure thee on
to extricate the painted floor
with face of man, painted red
and written with angry word,
hanging downward towards the past,
while audience awaits thee.
Yet no snack hath been set for thee.
In thy absence no chair saved for thee
to sit, back beyond the range of ear,
to smile at thoughts your own
and such magic as none hath seen,
for beauty lies within the heart of each man,
and waiteth for proper pen to freedom see
and bring tears to man's eyes,
as none be such other, save pepper pure
or onion cut, and binding eye and heart,
do cut clear, to smile within and reminisce
of friends lost to time and tradition.
Come hear me out
for sleep ye will on the morrow,
when helpers two are at thy bidding.
Gift of association to thee I give
with no more thought than thou hast given
what thou doest now – to freedom seek.
More still more I share with thee.
Friend in silence from other time and place

so far as would strain the mind which imagined such.
Those words bear magic –
No mere letters strung for eye to see,
but magic beneath the page.
Tarry not – lest exhausted be to greet thy day,
Yee of little endurance.
5:41 a.m.

Adieu, Robin

Darius Owen

April 22, 1996

Blur not the line tween peace and war
as once did Darius Owen.
Kilts held high, 'neath crimson sky
quilted orange between the line
twas mark of family line of Owen.
Small specks of white next gray lines of fury twill
worn 'neath bended knee of Owen's guild.
Farmers first, then men of iron.
'Twill last of all the kin o' Darius Owen.
Sacks of grain high in barn.
Horses none but ducks aplenty.
Still knives of knaves cut throats too.
These the kinsmen be of odious Darius Owen.
Couple oxen, bear and yoke of men.
Haulage of water to parched throats
both of cattle, man and geese did Darius and clan
to keep at bay the winds of winter
till spring thaw mark cadence
with fork and tine, to greet morning sun.
Clear yonder field of grain and bri
twas mark of Darius Owen.
With blood and thunder
as Darius clan slew, that what grew

in hill and dale of Larkin County.
None that grew from such tainted soil
couldst make escape from Darius Owen.
Who with smile and blade uncut
didst killed three family, friends and all
to covet not that barley field
which now lays bare
for idle eye to squint at piles of rock
so barren that not man or beast would want.
Tis tale of Darius Owen, long since dead
Spit upon this deed and head
of deadliest Darius Owen.
Small wonder that nothing grow
from hill so strewn to rocks and bri.
Tis justice sure for kith and kin
of now dead Darius Owen.
5:33 a.m.
Tis Robin Queen of night,
for daytime finds thee much indulged
in quest for such small pittance
that laughter not come
for tears so fluid, make me sad
as none such other canst write so clear.
Alas time is near for thee to rob yet another day
from thy purse so bare.
Talent such as yours, so rare

that heaven know not whence it came
nor why thee squander such as these
on objects small and white.
For men are creatures not of thought
but site and sound, of waste and want.
Wouldst thou engage me thus for time suspended be,
while with thee such fun as hath I not known.
Again I bid thee farewell till rested be
from yet more squandered time.
5:47 a.m.

Adieu, Robin

April 24, 1996 @ 12:36 p.m.

In great admiration do thee write
upon the page so blank.
Yet nothing comes forth which lures thee
deeper into oblivion but solitude,
creaking drawers and creaking vanes.
None other blows southward
but from death do eclipse thine eye
and heart as ancient ship upon the sea
in plight creaks to and fro in frost of night,

to awaken by light of day
to yet another mile to go.
Further still with sign not of end of voyage.
A plight so sinister that none hath told.
So bury ships in ancient ports and listen close
as spoken not as tiptoe small mice from ancient shore
to venture naught lest prize there be of gold
or coin of other lineage
to square the jib against its mast
and listen solitude for thine own ear.
Come hear this tale as spin it be
flapping 'neath breeze of night
to peril soul in tribute to scholarly lust
which be not thine enemy.
Tis tale of olde n' friends of olde.
Small stones piled not so high
as to bend windward storms of rain, sleet or snow.
Yet those same stones cast down upon the square
didst coffin not nor graveyard make
but piled enough to cut friend from foe
till death by poisoned arrow sow.
Pit friend to friend and foe to foe
till mixed up be they all.
Trust not thy party for friend or foe.
Know ye poison neither
but only indulgence with little else.

Mind in desperation wanders so
with little left between the lines
but grace and little there be of that.
Tomorrow may yet seek thee out
from shelter leeward of piled rocks.
So cast not another against thy neighbor
lest those samed be cast down upon thy head and knee
which thrown in anger doth return again to thee
which would in mind smile.
Spit not back lest thy words be et by thee and thine
so bitter that tongue in cheek will not suffice
to cover all thy family vice.
Seek not approval. None such be forthcoming.
Treat each encounter as saint or brother
for all are such in spite of mother.
Reckless be some but none such as kills his brother
for lust of money, saddened beyond grief.
When winged thing doth alight upon thy forehead
smile not nor look thee at thy neighbor
for lust comes from within and no other.
Small creatures lure thee out
into night without protection.
If wise thou wish to be,
share not a single thought with cowards
whose teeth grip tight the world's eye
with groups of blinded vermin.

Share not these small creatures,
creations of your thought
lest blind men poke out thine eyes
and call thee brother,
which have they not,
nor sister with which to sleep
but only each other in great disgust
which no man should endure.
Admonition as such given
I bid thee goodst night
and wish thee well upon the morrow.

Horace

April 25, 1996 @ 12:20 a.m.

Twilight calls from the end of time.
Tomorrow knows not whence it came.
Only yesterday hath honor among fools.
Nay, tomorrow shall cease its endless march
when man dances no more his jig.
Birds still sing in adulation
and worms creep forth to steal a leaf at night
but care they not for such as we

who cease our jig
to bide once more the end of line
and lineage small of clan and kin
when stops the clock by virgin calls
to destiny absolute.
Such petty knaves are we of man.
12:28 a.m.

By me, Robin, Queen of night

Dr. Brye

April 26, 1996 @ 2:48 a.m.

Small minded, he who cut thy toe
in admonition for payment.
Unrepentant for such foul deed,
his name in infamy resides.
A clown as such with such small mind
and clumsy hand canst heaven oblige.
With leeches small and toads a few,
didst make thy rounds among the poor
with gripe and dengue.
Cut he still with hand so clumsy,
fever followed with his tension.
None such other as Dr. Brye
shouldst in Hades lie
with beasts of burden and men of frock
who poison, kill and maim the flock
of he who came to lead all home,
where oncet lived we in all.
Surely such a man as this
doest deserve the flame of heaven's heel
for such competence he lack
to treat dog or bine.
Yet oncet his hand touched mine,

but in passing, twas I sick as never fore,
until death stood closely at my door.
Fortnight less or more 'fore his touch of hand
did leave me weakened, but dead not.
Curse that name Brye.
Bury him in flame
to resurrect at Hades door.
With naught to quench the flame,
but leeches few and pain many.
Icarus in crossing had not the plight
such as those touched by hand of Brye.
Surgeon to sow.
Whence he came of such lack of knowledge,
none can say.
But spit upon his gray stone
plenty there be willing
ev'n by day with priest in tow.
Such slough was he named Brye.
Spitted in eye by devil be.
Blinded to pity.
Burn his soul forever in Hades corner.
The curse of rattle and bones be less
than touch of Brenden Brye.
3:10 a.m.
To sleep I thee release.
One final curse afore I go.

Benefit to be upon family Brye.
Spit thee twice int' his eye.
Oncet for me, oncet for others.
Curses to his cousins also.
Such vermin of the staff
hath none such ever been.
His touch didst killeth me so young.
3:14 a.m.

Adieu, Robin of Loch–lore

Transcriber's note:
Apparently Robin had been treated by this Dr. Brye and subsequently died of fever before the age of eighteen.

To The Queen

April 27, 1996 @ 5:25 a.m.

Of such do I freely speak –
for of this Queen, nor for this Queen am I not.
Queens as such, can such good rulers be.
Not so the kings with wives a many
and brains a few and thoughts of trout
in constant mind but none the less
Queens too be given to squander and to lust.
Thus human be, to squander another's wealth
seems somehow less squanderous.
Queen of Night is small title taken out of context
and time from which it came.
Tis but game for me
but not so for those of time past.
To Queen was given life, lust and fortitude
as to none other save slut in whorey night
and fit of lust thus fallen.
Still – curse of Windsor be it real
not just bawter on drunken tongue
and saunter to and fro as possibility.
Any curse can cursed be but curse of Windsor own
be of such burden as few hath born
nor yet so long in coming.
More and stronger be curse of Windsor.
E'en in time yourn wilt thou view

the curse of Windsor full circle come
with demolition and such plight
as England dear hath not seen –
but bloodless in passing the House of Windsor
shall take its valid place in history.
5:38 a.m.

Lucille, Robin, Queen of Night

p.s. To see afore thought, is given thus the woman,
Lucille.
Tis but game I play to illuminate and to amuse.

Adieu

April 28, 1996 @ 4:33 a.m.

Born to suffering,
take not thy plight with serious thought
for tis but temporary lesson of sort.
Thy plight, a pitiful sight to some,
mere inconvenience to thee in reality.
Trust not the mind to trick thee into remorse.
Learn thy lesson well such that others need not.
So endure thy long hours of suffering.
Time well spent.
But seek ye out, not pain of discontent.

But seek ye, the light of wisdom.
4:40 a.m.
4:54 a.m.
Think ye little of consequences great
for arrogance as these will not rewarded be.
In haste as quick as any
for told by many yet still unheard.
Life is too quick.
Seal not thy fate so quickly.
Take time to plan thy destitude.
Make not allowance few
for altercation many may thee avoid,
'fore the close o' day.
Tis easy but to smile and kindness give.
Rather wouldst hanged be
as upside down from life's gaffle.
Think – then act not.
For having so acted wilst thou pay eternity.
5:07 a.m.
More I wish to speak, but record it not for tis private betwixt friends becoming. Nothing more will I speak till put thee down that pen.

Robin, Robin

Transcriber's note:
At this point we had a long conversation, none of which I recorded. It was very personal and most revealing.

April 30, 1996, 2:08 a.m.

Mourn ye not another day.
Someone dear to thee hast passed away.
Mourn thee not another day.
Unexpected be this death,
but eternity hath called.
Be not glad, nor sad at such passing.
Death to each in turn cometh
some sooner, some of late.
Once pass thee through that gate,
return ye not in liked form but as another,
with name and purpose other.
For hast thou finished current chore.
Weep not with this passing
for all that liveth pass away to life eternal.
Lest they seek again to return
as yet another child in coming.
Try to understand,
nothing hath thou lost but grain of sand,
which belongeth not to thee or to another
but to heaven from whence it came.
Not yours now. Nor never twas.
Passing story be complete.
For that short journey purpose unknown
but to him which planned its coming.
2:24 a.m.

Love, Robin

Pontius

5:40 a.m.

LUCRETIUS

Up, on the way.
Wait not the break of day.
The morrow be at hand.
Crisp, genteel, delight of senses be.
Pontius grows fatter with each passing day.
Sister, bring thy burden.
Town awaits those who follow ritual
and beat the sun to Barron's pass.

SILVIA

Brother dear,
tis not yet my time to bear child
but will be soon.
As such,
I dare not take thy bidding with serious delay.

LUCRETIUS

E'en old Pontius – fat though he be,
Canst lie 'n such condition large
and see not kinsmen and delights of town.

SILVIA

Go brother Lucretius.
Wait not for one so swollen with life's promise.
Take all in, but homeward be by sunset past,
lest Barron's rob thee of thy purse
'n perhaps thy spindly legs.

LUCRETIUS

Such as you would spoil fun of God's or men.
Onward, city fathers make way
for Lucretius hath parting left
Lazy sullen Silvia to childing burden.

GATE KEEPER (at the city gate)

Lucretius brother dear –
tis true that sister thine with child
be burdened – of unknown father?

LUCRETIUS

Nay. Was lazy Pontius fat and lazy
who thus did inseminate dearest Silvia
whilst she slept and dreamed she,
of porridge and pot pie,
which Pontius hath aplenty.

GATE KEEPER

None such swine as thee
dare enter city sweet
Of Pontius ruler be
with kings decree,
to cut thee down in very spot
where tongue as such doth indict thee.

LUCRETIUS

Tis but the sound of leaf against the tree
which heard thee.
Not a single word hath I spoke
to keep me from city gate,
denied of such excitement and savor.

GATE KEEPER

Enter thee of little brain
and much desire.
Yet hold thy tongue.
Lest Pontius cut it out
for old woman's prattle

5:57a.m.

May 1, 1996 @ 5:10 a.m.
(At Pontius' tower looking down over city)

PONTIUS

Wouldst thou this kitchen clean
from vermin such as roach and bine.

FLAVIUS

Beg thee pardon for such compliance
but must thee consume so much fowl?
Surely two or three be most adequate
for thy palate's savor.
Needest four or six to quench thy thirst?
Perhaps some wine to cut the flavor
and clean the mind from such endeavor.

PONTIUS

Mind not what few small fowl I doest consume,
for all within these gates be mine to order, eat or bail
E'n you, Flounder of king's court,
must bend an ear and knee
when doeth I come.

FLAVIUS

Only this small thing, I request.
Alloweth me to reside
until death do call me from thy side.

Shackle not thyself to other bride
or concubine,
lest they starve thee into submission.
Here amidst smoke and coal
till dust doeth claim me for its own,
here where tree and garden be most sincere,
familiar and friendly to mine eye.
Leave me yet to die alone but beg thee
cast me not out amongst the throngs
that teem thy city's wall
Here to rest amongst these coals.
That be my goal in life and in death.

5:27 a.m.

May 2, 1996 4:38 a.m.

Twix heéan 'n earth, lies region bare
where lies bones of men who didst not care
Them that's souls taste not life's pleasures
here twill rest decayed for time immemorial
Such thought as this shouldst spur thee on
to life to live and not postpone.
Characters populate this barren land
who waited whilst rest did live
Be not 'mongst these tortured souls
who waited, waited.

Now wait they eons in desolation,
desperate for chances lost
to abstinence and ascension.

CORNELIUS

Come brother.
Be thee fat among hogs and swine
yet related in blood thou art
and such as this cannot deny
that lovest not thou woman soft.
But quest thee only for the bone of men
of small stature and like delight.
Such be thou cook
who bake thee soup of dissolution
and prod thee from behind.
Keepeth thee so fat
that women do abhor thy belly
and thy touch and seek not thy prod
beneath such rolls of belly
lay hidden e'n to thine own eyes.

PONTIUS

Small brother.
Were thee not so larged be,
wouldst I poke thee in thine eye
with bone of chicken for such insult.

Tho be it true.
Nor women interest me not
for remindeth me of mother dear.
Bitch to the end.
Who poisoneth e'en water clear,
such that fish forget to swim
and drown in brine
as didst father mine.
Of such greed and bitches be of all women.
Cursed lie she entombed alone
with devil brother.
Both now dead from heads
lost to lust unfettered.
Dearest Cornelius, swine among men
who doeth spend all time with sluts 'n whore
as no man can name or recall.
Only thy large appetite for wine
canst keep thee healthy
among such vile creatures
who touch and paw with lack of penance
for what few coins that thou squander.
Thy rod will soon rotteth off
and be thee left only
with no small treasure
but only pot in which to pee.

5:05 a.m.

May 3 1996 6:13 a.m.

Morning greets thine eyes so sleep filled
as not to open without help.
Smoke from yonder burning brush
toiled by men of burden
to consume mountain whole till all is gone
e'en squirrel so precious
as to blind men's eyes from heaven sent
such message as to quell the tongue and feed the soul.
Blinded by such squirrel and tradition
unpracticed for too many years
such that none remembers what tradition is.
Pity be it that they see not past sunset
nor nose so near their face
that fly couldst land upon their eye
and see they not for sty so large
it fillith brain with pus of ignorance.
This smoke filled sky tis what sticks thine eye
so glued shut that water clean and warm
be thus required to open.
Yet see thee not thy luxury so fine –
raments many and food aplenty.
Take thee time to plant small roses,
cut grass 'n bend knee to nature most splendid.
Smile from thy heart.

Tis full with love yet untold.
Let not thy day be burdened
by such trivia as fill thy time.
Too soon thine eyes shine not more,
as all eyes do cease to shine.
Fill thy days with solitude, with friends true.
Squander not more time to worry sent.
Breathe slow with purpose and deliberation.
Un–grit thy teeth.
Clench not thy fist with fortitude.
Touch hearts you love with kindness. Smile for me.
6:31 a.m.

Robin, dearest

Transcriber's note:
There was a lot of smoke coming from the Catalina Mountains that morning when I got up. The Forest Service was conducting a controlled burn.

May 4th 1996 @ 4:47 a.m.

Pen to paper thus plied to,
I begin thee tell my pride whence I came,
no more I come,
for tis wasted effort which bore me thus.
Too many years didst I lie in anger

and in disgust at such lack of appreciation
and loss of friend that strange behavior didst emerge
till day which found thee by my side
with willing pen to do my bidding.
In thee hath I found friend lost.
With thy helping hand hath come
peaceful soul troubled not more
to incarnate again once more.
Be opportunity mine
but question now such intention.
With thy guidance and proliferation
such plan as this seem little worth.
So tarry by thy side for now
but seek yonder mountain bright
when obliged to move onward
with thought of little for earth's plights.
Begrudging not for that taken
by another as his own
now knowing tis of little port.
Pretentious was I that such trivia matter
when it doth not, when plied 'ginst the rule of coming
with losses little that seem so large.
In fact are irritations small and benign.
5:01 a.m.
Pontius – His tale and fortune – though misguided canst
wait the morrow.

Robin, dearest

5:59 a.m.
Pontius – dear Pontius –
didst not ride horse nor ass
for soreness was upon his own
by Flavius' proddings many.
Thinkest thou that man so blest
with fame and fortune,
known by many – loved by few –
couldst least of all be content
with normal posture
and not so given to bending over
to forget his mother –
though bitch indeed was she.

FLAVIUS

Dear husband – and bossed be,
though now content.
Doest want for yet more.
Tired am I from such thrusting
as be weak of knee.
If thou wisheth – more canst I give thee
with squash, carrot or with stick.

PONTIUS

Nay. Feed me now.
For canst I sit not for swollen be

that parched part
which calleth thee to my side.
Feedeth now tother mouth
which neither canst be satisfied.
Stuffed needing from both north and south.
Yet middle be not filled.
Touch me not with thy lips.
Draw this pustulance from my loin.
Wouldst that could I
but share such with woman.
To bare me thus child
to call upon in days to come
To kingdom give
and be content with dying.

6:15 a.m.

6:23 a.m.

LUCRETIUS

Silvia, dearest Silvia,
didst thou die barren and in pain,
with loneliness as thy brother and companion.
Float thee now with belly still swollen
in river cold and wet
from whence no child
nor nephew now shall come.
Such pain and sorrow shall I endure

for drunkenness and whoring
as none such other
through eternity and beyond.
Silvia I didst love thee
and whored so heavy for lust of thee.
Silvia most beauteous Silvia
sister mine which couldst have I not.
Even one small squeeze or knot.
E'en deaths grip
with swollen belly and bulged eye,
still such beauty as this calls me
to lust after thee.
Dearest sister thou hast died without child
and without knowing of my lust for thee.

6:31 a.m.

6:32 a.m.

FLAVIUS

Pontius, dearest Pontius,
here is thy child.
Stolen from drunken slut.
Whore to all of life.
Lusting for promise of such son most beauteous
as bears now thy name Pontius.
Pontius long liveth thee
and thy posterity.

PONTIUS

Thou shall be rewarded
for faith and duty
most appropriately.

May 6th 1996 @ 4:46 a.m.

MONSIGNOR

Come – Bind thy wounded soul.
Depart in peace brother.
Cling not to thy wicked ways.
Bear not false witness.
Surely confession now
will hasten thy parting
and fill thy future with paradise.

FLAVIUS

Nay. E'en in death
canst speak I not
of tribulation and greed
but Father dearest Father
give promise but one to me
who now quakes in death's grip.

MONSIGNOR

Death's last wish will we honor
if tis possibility for living to grant
to one so racked by pain and pustulance.
Confess thy sins.
Ease thy burden.
Ensure thy passage to heaven bound.

FLAVIUS

Nay. Such evil hath been done by such as I
that surely eternity be short to pay just dues
for all the pain which hath been caused.
Give dying soul some solace little.
Send brother thine to raise to completion
Son of Pontius whom now abandoned be
by one so weak and debilitated
that none can duplicate such folly.

MONSIGNOR

Have we such brother young, eager
and fit for service, such as thou doest request.
Lucretius shall be given to such task to completion
though burden great hath he of his own.
In such service to son of Pontius,
shall his penance and salvation lie.
Fear not Flavius for on the morrow

willst I commission give to young Lucretius
to bear thy burden
and raise son of Pontius in ways of truth,
wisdom and love for fellow man
as thou wisheth on death's calling day.
Fear not. Rest from thy burdens many.
Sleep in peace and quietude with almighty God.
5:07 a.m.

May 7th 1996 @ 4:10 a.m.

PONTIUS
What great service to this towne
and patrons near and far,
Brother Lucetius doeth thou for me.

LUCRETIUS
Tis but just service
for sins doth aplenty have I.
Each service to you and to your child
shall small payment be
for them committed –
most vile and wretched sins
as any man hath omitted
or confessed.

Fear not for such fervor
as now do I invest
that surely son of thine
will want not for any training
nor for love, nor patience,
nor kindness any.

4:18 a.m.

4:24 a.m.

Time hast not erased such sorrow
as still I feel in telling tale of lost Silvia
mine dearest friend, to such vile cursed man
as twas he Pontius of Shefford.
Thus I spit upon his grave and memory most wretched.
Time heals not that loss to me to mine heart
of dearest Silvia who in death bore such true
and wise a man as hast been ever born.
My tears doeth continue ev'n now for Silvia
lost Silvia so young and beauteous as any ever born.
Dearest Silvia still I love thee, ev'n now as before.

Thy friend, Sonja

Transcriber's note:
Sonja Sjorgensen was Robin's given name.

Michael, tis hard indeed to dredge up such memories,
to recall in testimony of such human deeds.

Just grant me one last moment to regain composure lost.
Today be thy friend's day of birth,
to remember or not, as suits thee.
Thy father too was born upon this very day.
Such incidence couldst be but coincidence.
Nay, none such as that exist.
Any man thinketh, that such do happen
plans of God and man are rare the same.
Of my life little hath thou been told.
In truest confession
I now share with thee of faithful hand.
Twas no small parting such as I to take
thus in death so young from friend and family.
Much was given, by father most caring
but too much was denied.
Schooling by tutor or friend was most denied
such that my greatest quest for means by which
conveyance of ideas small or large could thus be shared.
In his quiet desperation to contain such beauty
as none hath seen didst my dear father mine
deny to me any learning ev'n of kitchen ways.
Such that each day was passed in play
till play and lack of stimulation, didst prison make.
Death, such cruel parting, didst not liberate
but drove me in great despair ever harder
in search of one with whom to share ideas

lost to discussion tortured by freedom from articulation
thus was I imprisoned by father's love.
Such sadness motivate me to outlet find
whose hand that wrote as yours
in passing for my pleasure.
Found was he who admitted not
my knowledge of effort to communicate.
Great thanks and admiration for thy willingness
to investigate such strange phenomenon
as any hath encountered.
To forsake sleep and adulation for kindness thus offered
to one un–living such as I.
This kindness shall be rewarded and not forgotten.
4:55 a.m.

With love and admiration, Sonja Sjorgensen
Dearest, Robin

May 8th 1996 @ 2:02 a.m.

Dearest Mine. Thank thee much
for thy attention most becoming
for thy patience and story mine.
Thus to be told to you and perhaps others
willing to hear of one such as I

denied from birth by father most loving
any hope or promise to such express thought
or expression in vain attempt to keep hidden from me
evil ways or solitude in such quest
to keep forever young his child most becoming
he didst condemn such beauty to torment
and remain to this day most beauteous
but silenced in life from speaking
ev'n as do now I freely speak
with aid of your pen most affectionate.
Stifle not thy spouse nor child lest doomed be they
awaiting liberation through eternity.
Again thank thee much do I.
2:12 a.m.

Robin, friend in death as none such had in life.

PROVOST

Hear this man out.
Hear his tale of woe.
Lest thee too shall lie in damnation
for such lust as his of sister most beguiling.

LUCRETIUS

From day of birth wast I cursed as none other
to mourn daily for love forbidden.
Twas sister mine, none other
for such love had I for lust forbidden
didst I abandon faith in folly
to live in brothel mongst whores and worse
to emptiness, given to drink and debauchery
Such tale as mine share freely with thee
to lessen such chance of folly
of friends and patriots such as thee.
Bear not false witness gainst thyself
in hope of disbelief.
Abandon unbridled lust
in favor of service to God and King.

2:21 a.m.

May 9th 1996 @ 2:30 a.m.

When young was I, a boy did meet
with cheerful face and smooth skin
who came daily to thus converse and carry on.
Quite young was he perhaps of eight years no more.
Quite innocent but filled with wisdom

beyond his years
Long observations he did share
with seemingly no care
of lunch or other boyish activity.
Much did he teach to me about ways of earth
and views of men.
Never oncet did e'en I think nor question possibility
that perhaps he was not of this earth
but angel sent to help me in my solitude.

2:38 a.m.

2:57 a.m.

When noticed I his clothes the same
did he arrive each day
and questioned him of same
did he then arrive in most splendid attire
with nothing like any I had ever seen.
Such beauty and imagination as none would believe.
Madness, laughter, was this revelation denied
by Papa and maids alike.
Such sadness at their rejection didst I share
with my dear and trusted companion
In sadness and humiliation
did he admit to angel being.
What feared he most for our relation
was ridicule by elders which did disturb me
for knew he well that age of reason

and disbelief did approach us
when such friend as he
could no longer be
in accordance with tradition given.
But on that day in desperation did I bequeath,
did I vow that none such tradition as this couldst,
wouldst mark our passing upon wish of death.
Smiling he remained true friend as any
none the better hath I known e'en till my passing.
3:08 a.m.

Robin, friend of friends

May 10th 1996 @ 2:51 a.m.

In mourning loss of sister dearest
and only child of her own,
Lucretius enforced creative powers
thus engaged but few hath known.
To wisdom see from darkest hour,
tis gift of desolation from within.
Depth of vision cut clean through situation
to instill young Pontius such cleverness
and insight few of living sorts be given
In return did great appreciation young Ponti
show to brother Luci as was he known

since child was small and spoke but little.
E'en as he grew didst name remain for him Luci,
Brother Lucretius though formal was his name.

PONTI

Luci dearest Brother of church divine.
why hast thou given so much inspiration
and fine advice to heap upon my mind
with no thought of thine own needs or wants?

LUCRETIUS

Twas thus ordained by heaven
to see through these growing pains
and fever of lust and debauchery

PONTI

Still some needs of other things
must thou surely want.

LUCRETIUS

Nay. My one remaining lust in life
is for thine eyes to open be unto wisdom.
Love's touch from God most sublime.
For many, wisdom hath they not nor want of it
for interference with other desire.
In that absence you must assist
those of lesser mind to self destructive ways.

Give freely, in love of what is now freely given thee
through God's own vassal
Bear no guilt for this gift
so freely given and freely accepted.

PONTI

In humble grace do these gifts be accepted
from giver such as thee most beloved Brother Luci
God's greatest gift in friendship to me
in place of mother most absent.

3:15 a.m.

May 11th 1996 @ 3:26 a.m.

In desperation did he come. Whence goes he?
None canst say with certainty, whence he goes.
Few care, even none. But few will weep his parting.
Pontius, meanest governor as any, doth part
for damnation sure and judgment certain.
With his passing comes new and different rule
by one so young.
Inexperience hath its price
as doeth ignorance, lust and greed.
Pontius hath died, long live Pontius.
May his kin be most wise and forbearing

given to kindness, 'stid of lash.
3:33 a.m.
Time hath not softened such heart as his
which now must face judgment for wily ways.
Spit upon the grave of one most unpleasant
and e'en mean who tis told but often
was greatest fag which ever crawled upon God's earth.
Such painful death was surely most well deserved.
He who sat in power but ruled with own passion not.
May his soul rot for want of affection,
in solitude and desperation.
From this day forth to eternity
thus committed with duty not
nor caring any from such as we city dwellers
and burdened heavy with unjust tax
and worse by far, unjust rule.
3:40 a.m.
Thus do we the people commit in passing
this most unwanted servant of evil way
to his just reward on judgment day.
Most becoming son Ponti
must from this day carry forth rule of city
thus given in passing to one so young
and untested by deed or by decision.
Long live he who shall reign heir apparent
to city most splendid as any – Rome itself.

May 12th 1996 @ 4:02

When young was I, perhaps seventeen,
No, younger still at sixteen.
A small key was given me by friend most dear.
No words were spoken, just small key of green hue
filigreed as one such as only you have seen,
but never four, such many be unheard
That key of gold most perfect in shape
with purpose one to bind two hearts in friendship strong
as canst be broken by death nor evil deed.
Such now I give to thee in friendship pure and strong.
None such as this have been given ever by me
to mortal man – living nor dead
but such syncope with heart and emotion
is none but few in this life or after.
Perhaps twas planned,
arranged by some large hand that binds universe
with time apparent, which exists not,
but mere illusion be.
None the less, this key is freely given
to thee most splendid person
to bind us over great dimension.
Other keys, thee I see, are most equivalent
and bind thee through eternity

to others most precious.
Proud man should thee be
for most have none such keys – ever.
E'en after lives a many and trouble much,
deserve thou these and many more.
Be thy not of this world where now thy toil
and desperation be vapors of imagining.
These keys are real and beyond destruction
cannot be purchased for any price
never sought but of immense import.
These are the tools of creation, which builded universe.
Same as thinks most solid
but nay even universe so vast and grand
be nothing more than imaginings
of that one great source, which all are part and parcel.
That one God of all creation each mere speck of total self.
These keys cannot be taken nor freely given
but by purity and revelation.
All see them from a distance
and know them instantly, without spoken word.
Be not afraid for thine essence.
Think not with mind so fine and wit so cutting
but use that heart and soul most magnificent
to give birth to such things enduring,
trust – kindness – caring or inspiration
to instill in minds most vacant and wanton.
Use thy magic power freely

to contain rage most unbecoming.
Thinkest anger not
for thine anger pierces men's souls
to bleed them dry through time and eternity.
Thinkest thou to be simple man.
Nay creation is in thy hand.
Use it most wisely.
4:33 a.m.
Robin of Whettorne – most beloved friend, returning on the morrow as timing doth allow

Transcriber's note:
All of these titles or names of places, which accompanied Robin's name had some meaning or relevancy for her but I never really understood what they were.

May 13th 1996 @ 4:07 a.m.

Add not burden to the donkey's back
beyond that which prudence demands.
Be the load real – be the load imagined.
Yet still the burden thus perceived by man or beast
there in lies the true weight upon the ass
or sow or wooden plough.
What one chooses to believe
what one believes be true and fair

there in lies the burden for that creature.
Save not the plow for animal large
but for that which balks not at such tedium and slough.
Thus spake Ponti beloved Ponti
Belov'd by all for wisdom rich and heart so fair
None such other born to lead
hath men seen before or since.
No wanton greed nor lechery
couldst thou find in such heart of bestial man.
Twas gift of God thus transformed by Lucretius
as penalty of penance thus self imposed
in ignorance till dying day
Onward didst he pursue perfection,
in ward foreign but foreign not
for was family own son of Silvia
dearest Silvia most beloved,
which unknowing he didst sire in drunken lechery
born of secret lust by he Lucretius
father true to Ponti
greatest leader ever born – even yet
None such other will ever be
Ponti beloved ruler of Rome.
4:21 a.m.

Key # 1 *Gift of water – gift of life*
Key # 2 *Gift of trust*
Key # 3 *Gift of long suffering*
Key # 4 *Gift of love and devotion*

With these keys canst thou do many splendid thing.
Use them wisely.
These four keys can open any door:
Door of knowledge Door of wisdom
Door of deception, health or reason.
Any door can thus be opened
but by use of keys such as those given.

Transcriber's note:
These four keys are gifts, which have been bestowed upon me by persons living and dead whom I shall not name, to be used for the benefit of all. I guess I better figure out how to use them.

May 14th 1996 @ 4:23 a.m.

Tale most tempting hath been told
of long dead persons now long since cold

Embraced by earth's cold touch
but nay only dead to time
for live they yet and carry on
as though were yesteryear.
Yet we perceive them not but few as ghosts
do witness such strange comings and goings.
Chills the soul to disbelief
Till dead themself from life's last curse.
4:28 a.m.
Continue not this train of thought,
for wisdom doth call thee to her side.
Bear with me but moments few
to share thoughts of tenderness.
Smile – infectious as the wind.
Life's too short and death be long
Forever is such enduring form
Quiet thy spirit for restlessness.
Hear my gentle word written in solitude.
Cast in sea most turbid with disarray.
Currents carry across the void
memories yet vivid as life itself
unchanged by such long years in lonely solitude.
Keep thy contact open.
Channel such caring thoughts for thee,
for all that still liveth.
Life tis but moment frozen in time
once liberated doth time evaporate.

Great delusion of mind so enduring.
Bear toil and trouble
for life knows no other.
Soon – too soon – that door closeth
to open not again for any to savor.
Seek solace in solitude from life's wretched callings.
Daily shall I wish thee well in thy endeavors
at becoming person most complete.
4:42 a.m.
Again I bid thee Adieu, farewell for yet another day is dawning.

Robin of Rosequist

May 15th 1996 4:26 a.m.

Dearest Michael,
Thou hast been most accommodating
of such great assistance
with proscribing thoughts sublime
Complement now for most fine effort
as these are freely given by friend indeed.
Print these brief encounters
at great risk to thy reputation
for none there be which canst follow
or to rely on such futile chatter

as doth daily fill these pages with such ease.
Most helpful hath such conversing been
for one so locked in desperation
but now far better am prepared for new adventures.
Peace of mind hath thou allowed for one such as I
to share thoughts most jumbled for such time immense.
Thus in sharing now feel better off
for having thus so shared of the most disconcerting.
Thanks to thee most personal in nature.
Upon thee now doth I bestow, most graciously in parting.
4:50 a.m.

Robin of Redford – dearest, truest friend

4:54 a.m.
Letters thus written share such nature in common
as place from whence came such thoughts in writing.
Thus Robin of Redford,
towne small but most becoming.
Ev'n now tis such delight to visit,
though changes many hath thus occurred
since my parting.
But Brigadoon as concept doeth exist
for each and every towne and location
thus bound and frozen in grip of time.
On such occasion most appropriate,
canst towne most complete resurrect.

In same location or another for duration
such as one could view such happenings
long since parted, bound in timeless past.
Any disengaged or fear ridden slave of time
couldst hap upon such resurrection of action
and think themselves most bizarre
and even lost of mind and sensibility.
Even thoughts of others can condense
into reality if emotion driven.
Vision and hearing are such frail accouterments
that ill prepare thee for reality in truest form.
5:07 a.m.

May 16th , 1996 @ 4:59 a.m.

Charity – born of plenty
Greed – born of envy
Wellness – born of kindness.
These things all men know. Yet heed not
till kingdom call or death doth yawn.
Curse not another.
For in thy curse lies thine own undoing.
Rules not are these,
mere suggestions from deaths other side.
Oncet passed, ye cannot recall arrows shot,

or shot not but accept in likeness
all that thou hast cast against thy neighbor
and ginst friend alike.
5:04 a.m.

These brief interludes tween wake and sleep
be most convenient to dispatch any
that needs be transported through portal
such as exists this moment
joining spirits separated by distance
and dimension most unimagined
yet seemingly thou hast knack for such impossible task
as none other known by me or others
finding such difficult situation in which
no living soul hath interest
or commission to thus engage.
Most remarkable in passing art thou
of message most articulate.
In darkness doth thou see.
In silence doust thou hear.
In quest for knowledge thus forbidden to living souls
hath thou acquired most interesting skill
of commission most deliberate
and worthy of such punishment
as wouldst thine neighbors freely heap upon thy brow
if opportunity at such occasion should present.

5:14 a.m.
Upon this final page record most accurately
by my request that thou
hast achieved most remarkable achievement
as none doth appreciate nor never will
till death doeth take them far from familiar rule
where little hath they prepared and less understand.
Summon all thy kindness for them
that would cut thee to thy bone
and quarter thee most quickly
to abandon thee to fiery death by burning
for care they not to know of consequence most horrid
for each wayward deed most selfish
from whence all evil doeth come
launched 'cross time to descend thus again
to crush life and pleasure from all that so doeth.
None escape – none –
ev'n half wit 'n concubine shall share alike
in such unimagined folly for such passing trivia.
Tis thus sadness is born.
Perpetuated and again reborn
to terrorize living and dead alike.
Woe – oh woe to evil doers.
Tears and blood to come.
5:25 a.m.

Loving thoughts, Robin

May 17th , 1996 @ 2:30 a.m.

Soul – center of the universe
from whence all things are formed
not so t'other way as wouldst thou thinkest.
Nay all things solid come from stuff of mind's creation
No such thing – object of imagination exist outside
of presence of generation by mind,
most agile creator of universe whole in its entirety
that which flashes momentarily into existence
then exists not at all
to return again with next pulsation from distant source
from whence al things derive their engine.
2:26 a.m.
No safe haven be there from such gyrations
that spindle all existence
Ev'n now as you write blink ye on and off
and on again with such quickness and regularity
that thinkest thou of no discontinuance.
Be there such same gyrations are stuff of all.
None be which is not same.
Pity those bound with thoughts of realness and duration
None such as this doth exist – only be imagined –
Frozen solid by time which itself doth not exist.
2:33 a.m.
Strange but true, Robin of Yorkshire, most beloved

5:46 a.m.
Surprise not thy taskmaster.
Urge thee on to thine own destruction.
Calm be the sea before storm doth descend
upon troubled waters.
Thy sheep be many and most agile and fatten well.
Graze them not on thy neighbor's grasses –
for theft of ev'n grass
canst bring thee down to knee so burdened.
Mongst thy neighbor's herd be poisoned breath
which spreads most quickly to ruin herd entire.
Avoid ev'n visit on that land
lest poisoned be thine own herds.
Look to north – to headwaters clear and clean.
Avoid sullen waters with sulfurous smell
and taste that bite thy tongue and poison thine herds.
Twill pass as all great tragedy and mishap must.
Time cleanseth all save rotted soul
and fresh pasture shall return again.
5:57 a.m.

Robin of Isle of Mann
Greet this day with confidence and guile.

May 18th , 1996 @ 4:42 a.m.

Robin of Luxford brings wishes for a fine day,
as fine as any thou hast ever had.
Many mind most splendid hath labored hard
to overcome such weakness
as imposed by human mind,
which though marvelous be it –
still blind to truth and reality.
Such contrivances hath man tried
to engage worlds beyond naked eye and bare hand
yet nothing hath been thus devised
to overcome such shortcomings
as imposed God upon nature of man.
Intuition and quietude be best of tools
as humans hath devised.
Both of little or none in scientific value
but such device canst thou contrive
which alloweth any man to view fate
from comings as well as goings.
Such device be possible to contrive
with materials at hand.
To fly from earth's bounds
and human frailties into realm yet unknown –
but merely imagined of.
No mere machine –

but in complexity and function
doeth require insight and understanding.
4:54 a.m.
Container quiet be not required –
but solid control of emotion must absolute be.
For death and destruction awaits one
who alloweth emotion any to shadow such travels far.
Training little will assist in such skill in such control.
Distorted mind be death's second curse.
Bring not emotion, nor distortion of mind
from drink or potted flower.
Foreign substance bind mind to some unyielding belief
and curse the user to death most certain
or casted mind thus forever un–working.
Soft liner neither be required – nor chair –
nor bed upon to lie.
Separate thy spirit pure
from chafing body thus enclosed.
but leave behind thy dwelling place in security
so that none steal from thee in thine absence that vessel
from which thou must returneth or perish
as all that liveth do cling in desperation
past time of usefulness.
Hesitate not lest thou be lost to time and reality
from whence thou never returneth.
Stray not from thy purpose certain.

Go quickly for deviants returneth not
but crash upon sides absorbent
and be thus absorbed into other time and place.
Turn not towards the tube of travel
lest all should be lost.
Only one essential skill be thus required,
to remember.
Amnesia be blessing and be curse
but separation most certain
from all that is and isn't.
Give up thy burden of amnesia.
Give up that which hath thus enslaved all mankind.
Fear not for in so doing willst thou be most enlightened
to compensate for such fate
as man hath thus been burdened.
Sanity be name most given for burden of amnesiac.
Enlightenment be thus comprised of loss of amnesia.
Ticket most splendid to unfettered travel.
5:18 a.m.

With most loving thoughts, Robin

May 19th, 1996, 2:51 a.m.

Born thus again to curse the waters –
from whence all creatures came.
Born thus again to creep forth from time forgotten
to bind the spirit and mind
as one small ball of clot
with spittle and with sap
with sunset and tears
with blood and forgotten memories
from time since long lost.
Open not thy eyes for fear of seeing him
for oncet twere thou, evil doer
and curse of brine succor
of sap from young tree
Swine among men twere thou
Born of great strength and burden to many
Yet ev'n now remnant of thy past self
doth sometime creep through to surface sweat
with such anger and such rage
that barely canst thou contain such evil doer
as thou oncet twere.
Compassion seeming be camouflage at best
for long lost beast which lies within each man's heart.
Heart of yours be most black in antiquity
Soot from bygone days when lesser restraint

didst thou show to all men great and small.
Upon thy death must thou be preparedest
to once more face thy past selves
from whence this life was born
with penance most upward in thy mind,
with purpose most specific
to care for most feeble and most vulnerable
to give hope to child of men
who care not for thy offspring.
Thus such great caring and admiration
wast born of thy past where mercy absent
didst thou freely roam to terrorize both beast and man
with vengeance such as now be not known nor practiced
ev'n by most brutal and uncaring Iraqi and Chinese.
Breathe slowly and breathe deep
for thy time has not yet come to meet thyself,
pain in death's struggle.
3:10 a.m.
Robin – Most trusted friend in death and life.

May 20th 1996, 4:55 a.m.

Whence time flows more slowly than before
this be vortex of creation.

Pull down this slowing upon thy self.
Surround thy dwelling with such fog
till time ceases its endless tick.
In this vortex lies birth of all emotion.
Here lies each pattern for life's creations.
Shatter nothing for in so doing
wilst thou break creation's engine
for that which has been broken and be unfixed.
Build thy own mold.
Channel emotion– most of all pure love into such pattern.
Unmold thy self to discover new dimension
new direction and boldness as none such other hath.
This be secret to all things that liveth and be reborn.
5:03 a.m.
With fervor and conceit, nothing be forbidden,
nothing be lost but effort unmade.
Thou canst do most splendid things,
if thou wilst, only if thou wilst.
Such meager thoughts be wasted not on thee
but practiced each day even now
knowest thou that each small child doth teacher make.
Slowly thou doest learn –
from each such child learn more small truth –
till picture clear of thy potential.
Waste not energy on worry.
Focus total attention on each small child.
Learn lesson well – till thou canst stop thy world at will

to thus embark pon adventure most intriguing –
upon quest for that which be unthinkable to mortal man.
Turn to face each day with excitement
and envy for what shall come.
5:17 a.m.
Find thy own pattern. Re–visit it.
Turn back the clock.
Change thy purpose and function at will,
Yet knowest thou that such meddling
can cause failure as well as great success.
Dwindle not thy days in search of eternal life.
For be that now –
part and parcel with whom thou art.
Come carry with thee such merry thoughts
of time spent with friends – and laughter.
Dwell not on past misgivings.
Tomorrow has its birth in seeds of today and yesteryear.
Plant for tomorrow's harvest this day
and every moment will fill with such splendor
as few doeth know.
Yet seek in solitude that place
where time doeth stand still.
Try thy hand at creation – of self and other.
Re–arrange such troubled minds such that smile again.
Youth be but fading fancy to child of man –
but perception of youth and lasting vigor
cometh from within.

Close not such window by convention.
Keep open such possibility as do I present.
None such other hath shared with thee such secret
of activity so worthy and so great.
Knowest thou that these words be true for small child.
Any such small child will attest to truth
and veracity of whence I speak.
Child at heart – even now art thou.
Open that window which others would have thee close.
Open imagination and creation.
5:25 a.m.

Robin, Friend from beyond death's door
Doeth bid the farewell for yet another day.

May 21st 1996 @ 3:40 a.m.

Thundering 'cross time comes echoes
of carnage long forgotten.
Thus spoke Theraseuth to children of bygone time
Not in idea but in error – in action.
Evil today was born of lost pain and suffering like none known now– ev'n in war and famine.
Seeds of such wanton destruction
were cast upon the sands of time, now to sprout

and bring forth blood lust, violence and debauchery.
Not so twere always.
Time oncet were where all men were brothers
in actions and in thoughts.
The glut of evil overtaketh them.
3:47 a.m.
Curse not man for evil deeds but curse evil itself
which doth perpetuate crime by violence and disgust.
Weep not for lost and stolen stuff,
for of such sorrow be born lust
for violence gainst fellow man of lesser means.
Such lust be not satisfied till sons of sins and evil doers
be mixed with blood and sweat to tears make.
Women of the world weep not for thy lost sons
for none be lost – ever –
but consumed by hate and evil ways
perpetuated by bygone days.
All waste – all want – all evil thoughts
Tis pity such as none doth understand.
3:52 a.m.
Thus spake Theraseuth.
Thus poured sands hour by hour from glass stubborn
that only hand of God canst cease its endless tumble.
3:55 a.m.

Robin of Knox – Dearest friend as any thou knowest

Mine hand so soft doth reach gently cross time
to touch thy brow.
Fear not nothing,
for thou wilst prevail in admiration,
knowing first hand that thy time be nigh
when blessing of God be upon thee.
Man canst giveth thee little in way of comfort.
Live life each day to its fullest.
Regret not thy words.
Be kindest even to thy self.

4:58 a.m.
Tale of passion – tale of woe –
tale of child born of lust –
not of prudence and of planning.
Thus hath city streets been filled with such children
as these wanted not nor never twere.
Pity as great as any canst befall one from another
gift of life given with sustenance not nor caring any.
Streets piled high with human litter,
with ignorance and despair.
Crimes as these go not unpunished.
Victims to the end – in lust for love long lost –
love never had.

Thus is human bondage so perpetuated
by one generation upon tother.
That such ignorance as these be allowed–
nay encouraged by claims of government to be –
shall bring even great nations to their knee –
in such sorrow and such strife as any couldst allow.
Where morals not doeth reside
is where evil doeth reside.
Evil be not more than lack of caring – lack of love.
Nothing more be required for seeds of evil to abide.
Time pours forth such tales of woe –
self inflicted to the end.
Ignorance – ignorance be not bliss
but curse of uncaring – curse of greed.
Time will wash all gratitude from thine hands.
Time will bury thee in its end.
5:12 a.m.

Thus spake Theraseuth to such children lost.

Malchur

May 22nd 1996, 2:41 a.m.

FATHER

Cast out these evil spirits.
Bind not thy spirit to this molten gold.
Escape now with thy life
and condemnation lost but thus given.
Bind not thy soul to this molten gold
for cursed shall it be for eternity.

MALEUS

Thus be my chance at eternal life –
filigreed – small shape of Christ
here will I reside, here bide my time.
Molten pot of gold
pour out such beauteous gold
for all to behold.
Bind me with thy purpose.

FATHER

Look to life amongst common believers.
Bind not thy soul and breath to this small pot,
to this liquid gold, most void of love –
with tiger's eye.
Look up, man.
Cast not thy lot with molten hues
of fire brazened gold.

House of Windsor thus in–trapped
by William – twas his name,
fool of fools to thus seek life in molten gold
frozen in time till once more liberated
by fire brand and furnace glow.
Fool of fools didst curse his house.
House of Windsor till it fall
by weight of Tierney from within.
Nay not even greed so egregious compare
to sheer stupidity of William of House of Windsor.
Such evil thus encrypted during mass
said so high and pontius
such foul odor of burning flesh
reeks still from such small icon
of casted molten metal gold.
Engraved from within by stupidity.
Engraved from without by lost soul of king to be.
Pardon, neither asked nor given.
Tales of secret still untold.
House of Windsor be thus filled to brim
with such weird tales as one of William
wrought in gold with spirit lost to lust for life eternal.
Such empty carcass did survive most high mass
and construction thus of frivolous icon casted in gold.
Nay, body of man alone was William's curse
mindless, speechless, sightless to end of life.
Hulk of once king to be, void of all intelligence.

Thus curse of Windsor be born
of each generation
till son of William lost doeth liberated be
by fall of Windsor and melting in such fire
of icon golden. Filigreed – unpleasant to eye and hand
of small Christ entwined at birth in golden manger.
Pity poor William once king to be
now in wait of fire to liberate soul
thus frozen most foolish in molten gold
congealed to shape of Christ and manger small
celebrated only at high mass at equinox festival
within secret chambers by priest lost to life.
Self– indulgent even to life's secret callings.
Pity – such pity to them all
e'en William – poor William – lost to crown.
Frozen in stupidity – frozen in time.
3:17 a.m.

Tis tale most true.
Most obliging, Robin of Oxford

A tale most compelling of single–minded lust for eternal life. That which be freely given to all men.

May 23, 1996 @ 2:44 a.m.

Small wings – delicate – immobile frozen in death's grip
so tenacious liken to glass blown by master artisan
thus all end their reign of terror ev'n largest of all.
None escape this world alive yet whole in passing,
whole in death as whole as any ever were in life.
Sounds lost forever yet be they heard
most precisely by ear most silent.
Words unspoken, sounds unheard yet understood
with such precision as ne'er couldst have been
on earth living in pain and deceit.
This be no mystery but fact so stated most emphatically
for thy pleasure and pleasure of lesser wisdom.
Wings frozen in time but liberated be they
in such splendor and perfection in God's court.
2:52 a.m.
Time deceitful time be not thine enemy
but mere measure of thy reality.
Tis of no consequence – none–
but enslave thee to its taskmaster
most easily with such fervor.
Such be folly thus born of men,
watched by men in ignorance of their true nature
which be timeless – stuff of stars.
What convincing doth thus be needed
to tilt thy eye and twist thy head

away from slavery thus attached
to motion most concentric and devoid of caring.
Folly – folly– with thy passing
from day to day be thy constant companion.
2:59 a.m.

Robin of Liverpool – Robin of Luxem – Robin thy friend

May 24th, 1996 @ 5:11 a.m.

Land – third element of the eternal triad –
sought by many – owned by few
belongeth to no man.
Respect life and all that liveth upon the land
thus created over millennia.
Ownership is of no consequence but mere illusion.
Even gravesite small and deep be not thine own.
Tarry not in quest for land
its ownership be but farce.
Wealth – second of the eternal triad be even less.
Waste not thy precious in quest of wealth
for it be even less than land in felicity.
Wealth be not only illusion
but also artificially assigned by culture and by group.
Waste not time – in quest of wealth
which figures not in eternity –

least of all endeavors –
burdensome destroyer of soul.
Power over others be least in triad of lust
Worst of all three but sought after most of all –
guarantees a lost soul.
Seek not power over others
for here in lies earth's greatest horror.
Human existence be not for power gained
nor power bought
but for appreciation of world most beautiful
of lessons most profound –
from whence new life and experience
most profound doth come.

Eternal triad – trap most cunning for unwary souls.
Seek yet another way.
Avoid eternal triad with great effort and disguise.
Seek freedom for thy soul.
Seek peace of mind and kinship true.
Avoid always bondage to eternal triad.
5:28 a.m.

Robin, plain and true

May 25th, 1996 @ 1:57 a. m.

Trust not thy values –
for they be not of creations own.
Still be they better than others
but not adequate to thy purpose.
New concepts be required
most urgent in their coming
lest thee believe untruly of thine own perfection
which hast thou not nor any man yet born
nor likely to yet be born.
List thy reasons for such strange perceptions
and be they left most wanton
in display gainst nature true
and perfection most splendid
which hast thou not.
2:02 a.m.
All know inherently right from wrong –
Best at birth but soon corrupted
by age advanced –
by teacher most corrupted –
thy parent and thy greed
for self–desire and self–satisfaction.
Look no further than thine own nose
for guidance and correction
for such tip of nares both contain respiration
and desired truths.

Focus thine eyes upon its summit
and be amazed at how strange direction
hath thou been convinced to follow folly
most extreme by convention – most surely induced.
2:08 a.m.
Corrupt not such wisdom with explanation.
Take truth as cometh it –
straight from creation to thine own nose.
Know that only such truth –sublime and most correct,
shall thus descend from heaven to thy nose
or nose of any so inclined to look at such with true intent
and not merely practice false observation
of prior conviction – boosted to realm of truth by deceit
most direct with raised brow and tongue beguiling.
2:13 a.m.
Truth can set thee free.
Lies but deceive thee and fellow man
who believeth in some strange book or tother –
when truth most perfect and correct –
dwell at tip of thy nose and tip of tothers
but choose they merely to look upon such splendor
in clear conscience and quietude
as be most recommended through eternity.
Follow thy nose to liberation
from human bondage and deceit.
2:18 a.m.

Love, Robin of whores, thy friend indeed

May 25th 1996 @ 4:03 a.m.

Life's lessons be long and many.
Attention to detail be thus required
of all who would avoid such returning
as times many and yet again many
till count be lost among waters most turbid
with experiences most varied and real.
Cast not thy soul away into such turbulent waters.
Seek ye the shortest course to escape possibility
of returning to face the switch of life's tortures,
pain and dying till blurred be
these visits many and bizarre.
Tempt not the devil's advocate or wilst thou see him
real as any known – upon thee settle
to kindle burning desire which welds thy fate
to returneth most certain again and again
until exhausted be thy attempts at escape.
Wait patiently for dawn.
Make no request of unknown.
Lie quietly in dawn's stillness
till descend upon thee clear understanding.
Bigotry be begotten in ignorance and strife.
Silence of thy internal clock can save thee much anguish
and suffering which both be needless
and waste of time and life's energy.

Small wonder such violence and distrust of all existence.
Small wonder that men hath devoured
so much of mother earth.
Lessons most grave hang in scales of balance.
All – all will be weighed in correct devotion
and returned to each according to his just deserving.
4:18 a.m.

May 26, 1996 @ 3:48 a.m.

Transfer thy wellness for misery
by dwelling on past problems.
Transfer thy wealth for ill health
by diet poor or meager.
Transfer thy good name for one of outcast
by small deceit.
Transfer thy soul to care of devils
by wanton neglect of thy spirits needs.
Transfer thy time for ill gotten gain.
Eternal bliss canst hardly equate to misery most severe.
Ask thyself each day before, after and during,
Is this food for my soul,
Is this fodder for my body,
Is this waste of life and time?

3:58 a.m.

Kind woman – show me thy injured soul –
such that by touch most delicate and unobtrusive –
wilt thou be once again the whole.
This gift thou hast been given –
Use it for thy gift be as such nothing – unused.
Child of poverty – pick up thine countenance.
Stand tall for thy parents gave thee life.
Ask not that they give more.
This world – this life be thy gifts.
Secure memories most separate for thy self –
For memories will be thy only companion in death.
Ask not for newness of cloth nor jewelry golden.
Such trinkets bind thy feet and cloud thy eye.
Liveth life.
Be not shackled to any man's theory.
Waste not thy time in search of penance for thy parent's lack.
Waste not thy precious life on envy.
Creature of eternal darkness –
turn thy face so perfect to windward and to lee –
to greet rising sun and moonlit eve –
crisp fall of driven snow by wayward winds
that call thy soul in search of small demons within.
Face each new task with zeal.
Be life's most devoted follower.
Let not thy poor beginning entomb thy spirit.

4:11 a.m.
Tis sadness great upon which be heaped – untold misery.
Such burden as parents pour upon unborn children
which seek nothing but fair start
at breathing such polluted air.
Blood of parent in contrast profound
be poison pure and certain to unborn mind
and body much injured by abuse,
by wanton neglect,
by disregard for life's single purpose,
to procreate yet another birth,
another possibility.
4:16 a.m.

Sleep my friend, Tis Robin of Wixel at thy side

May 27th, 1996 @ 3:33 a.m.

Morning breaks again –
from east to west arises the sun in endless fashion.
To assume that always hath this been so is naive.
Nay – nor will cycle continue as such unchanged forever.
Great opportunity for life –
frozen moment of time seem endless to our mind.
Drip by drip till all be lost in disharmony.

Slowly with doubt little wilst thy world change to briefly
hot then long suffering cold of great duration.
3:45 a.m.
Death by starvation –
Death by self–infliction –
Death by loss of spirit
Will to liveth do depart –
to return not for fourteen year –
to world most different –
to attitudes most changed.
Guns – knives – exploding rocks –all share –
but little in common with such disaster
as descends upon humankind
from ignorance of self discipline
and gross disobedience of basic decency
that such folly cometh with contagion
most virulent as none hath known.
3:51 a.m.
Pity be to living dead – dead of body – dead of soul.
Yet continue they to creep the earth
to spread contagion to woman man and child.
even to chicken most securely caged
till numbers of ill be more than illness not
till balance most precarious be thus reached
till family be extended to distant cousin
to seek burial by friend not nor enemy uncertain.

Life be no longer bearable to many
who seek refuge in self immolation.
Such folly doth come most certain.
3:57 a.m.

Robin

May 28th, 1996 @ 3:05 a.m.

Small chip of glass, which cut thy finger
was not glass nor even small
but bit of thorn from twig of rose
or thorn of fruit tree but cut the same
as though twere knife or shard of glass.
Such is life's limitations upon us heaped
by flesh and bone so frail
as to keep ev'n most nonchalant
in worry constant for fear
of cut or scratch or rend so small
as might allow death's grip to enter –
blood born parasite to end our days.
Such worry be of little consequence
to one so dead as I –
Yet liveth on as now I speak
as tho twere living ev'n now.

3:12 a.m.
Fear not for thy safety –
for when death does call –
little excuse be there for tarry.
Know thou this – as sure as any
that death's icy grip be most transient
and yield freedom complete
but with grave difference –
for thy deeds shall haunt thee – eternal.
Be not in hurry for closing of that door.
Build as many good memories and deeds
to see thee through the winter's long night.
3:16 a.m.
Tis easy to mend souls with kindness and afore thought.
Most difficult tis to mend such tare or rend
as evil deed hath made in fabric most elastic
to stretch from birth to death to eternity.
Rock slowly in thy cradle wooden or chair most squeaky.
Rock slowly for time doeth end and eternity begin
for thee as for all God's creatures.
Yet evil dog, be there none –
nor evil bird that ply the sky.
Nay only men among all earth's creatures be evil bent.
3:21 a.m.
Such weakling – such hairless freak
only men be bent on evil for evils sake.

Know thou this,
that ere death knocks twice upon thy door
to claim thy soul to eternity
thou hast chance aplenty to mend thy ways
and stock up for winter's long encampment
where solitude and desolation
need not be thy only companion.
Take flowers – take song – take good deeds aplenty
to step upon and line thy way cross eternity.
Tis well worth effort small.
Tis worth the time well spent –
and better taken than ignored.
3:26 a.m.
Such trivia be labour of love for thee
and ev'n for thy friends.
None there be who wish to hear of solitude
nor desperation but thing far worse
do reside in death's darkest hour.
Thing most horrible as none canst imagine
also wait for lost souls to devour again and again,
Eternal pain and anguish await,
the ill at heart, ill of will.
3:30 a.m.
Take thy leave – till the morrow if thou must
but go forth this day and all others as they last

to greet each fellow traveler as thy last
and best good friend.
3:31 a.m.

Love, Robin – again as always

3:48 a.m.
My father didst deny me in
love and desperation any schooling.
Thus denied any opportunity
to create writings or works of creation.
Yet could he deny me not these thoughts
which now recordeth thee
most effortless – thee doest for me.
In love and fear – parents close many doors
of opportunity for each child.
Such effort be misguided
for thy children be God's creations
not thine own property
to direct and misdirect at will.
Ev'n now – centuries since my father's parting
doeth his narrow foresight still impede.
3:55 a.m.
Mother dearest did'st I not know for death took her
from father's side soon after life began for me.
Thus great was father's consternation and concern
for child born of such trauma and such loss.
Still tis poor excuse to deny one's destiny

to thus cloister as he did in isolation –
though beauty filled
yet still denied opportunity to write – to compose.
Twere it not for thee and thine –
still my name would buried be
with waxen body now decomposed.
4:00 a.m.

Robin

May 29th 1996 @5:02 a.m.

Whilst thou slept and did dream of places far better –
didst I too dream –
for so composed is my world to be wholly dreams.
Yet when thou wakest – dreams vanish
to be thus forgotten till death.
Dreams do not end – nay
no escape be remotely possible for dreamer
from dream extrication be thus not possible.
Control of minds wandering is absolute in necessity –
for wandering mind doth soon encounter –
most horrid things of abject terror
as none such exist on earth
even with imagination most profound

and keen as yours hath been.
Dreams for thee – be most important
in reconciliation of days distress
and righting of disorder and disarray.
Yet for dead such as I, be they palate of creation
For dreams of dead men be ghosts
and shadows for those who yet liveth.
Endless dreaming be most unpleasant
for mind worse at management
of such fine curse and opportunity.
Whilst thou slept didst I dream thee here to my side.
Most compelling be thou strength of character
and thy wit yet troubled mind
didst make thy visit less a pleasure
and more a fit of unstable mind.
Get control of that wandering much –
Practice most diligently –
for upon thy day of calling wilst thou lack of discipline
in thought and deed be most upsetting
and of great disadvantage to thy purpose thus at hand.
528 a.m.
Upon returning from such journey from deposition
thus to country and terrain most unaccustomed –
confusion be most common.
Lack of concentration – be most profound –
but gather thy wits about thee.

Concentrate most fully on task
of simple, safe and pleasant location.
Focus vision, mind and hand till all work as one –
in compliance with minds command.
Then balance be returned.
So amble not in wobbling fashion
as would one given to much drink and adulation.
Still – most pleasant was for me to see first hand
friend of such determination
to thus extract most compelling thought
in such exactitude as doth make me smile
at thy accomplishment most splendid.
Still would nicer be to have thus been given opportunity
to communicate in written word while I too lived
and breathed as even now doest thou daily
in such disregard for days treasures –
abandoned in search of gold and copper coin.
Pity to see such waste of opportunity
in spirit so fine as thou dost possess.
Again I bid thee most splendid day.
Farewell do I bid thee not,
for on the morrow shall I return
as opportunity doth present itself.
5:41 a.m.

Most beloved friend, Robin

May 30th, 1096 @ 4:04 a.m.

Count not thy blessings gainst another's
for here in lie seeds of greed.
Blessings be no gift but tokens small amounting to little.
Blessings be they that alloweth coolness of thought
and slowness to anger – these be treasures true.
Golden bullion be of no value – none 'cept to coffer –
to sink a blind man who swimmeth life's stream.
Focus thy attention not upon stuff
but upon the stuff of stuff.
That be creation most interesting
and worthy of much diligence of effort.
Stuff be merely after birth.
Birth is creation true and kind.
4:11 a.m.
Admonitions abound –
yet heed thee little of which I share
message most accurate and correct.
Trudge on – trudge on –in blinded fashion
both eyes open yet seeming nothing to see –
nothing witness thou
but passage of yet another day unfulfilled.
Weakness creeps upon thy burdened shoulder.
Step back – look with open eye at thy condition.
Surely ev'n beast of burden be not as blind as thee.

4:16 a.m.
This day – today – is gift so great as none imagine
that be now dead and cold in covered clay –
or vessel gilded bright to decorate mantle filled with dust
and laden with useless stuff.
Grasp this opportunity golden.
Stop thy useless twitch – in favor of most glorious day.
4:20 a.m.
Tether not thine fine hand to ax or shovel.
Let thy mind wander most free.
Alloweth thy nose a smell of eternal bliss.
Plunge thy hand in cool water.
Marvel at mysteries most marvelous,
at life's most precious treasures.
Thou canst now nor ever please another with thy effort.
Please thyself with thoughts most pleasant –
With deeds most benevolent –
beyond thy mind's comprehension.
Small story wouldst now I share –
if thy pen doeth ink in abundance have.
Perhaps another day if time befall us
and casts me once again into darkest isolation.
4:27 a.m.
Small child of caring – didst I encounter long ago
when still didst liveth – yet attention little did I pay him
which sought me out, to be my most constant companion.

Every waking moment – he be with me –
lest I hide away in solitude to seek.
Each day – grew he stronger in my heart
till one day he cometh not.
Such great sadness did engulf me – even to this day –
emptiness most profound doth descend upon my heart
when any thought of him doeth occur.
Of such friendship is solitude and sadness born.
4:33 a.m.
His presence seemed most assured –
till one day he cometh not again.
Such is childhood – such is life.
One day death will descend and life will be no more.
Such sadness at opportunity lost – to touch his hand
that most curious child who's name I knoweth not
Nor any other saw his presence –
For that child was innocence –
That child was me before I grew old
and no longer could see life as magic–
life as living dream – of possibility, unlimited possibility.
Once past that time – once past that place –
childhood shall not return again.
4:40 a.m.

Robin

May 31, 1996 @ 1:24 a.m.

This be most adequate time to continue thoughts
as doth thou rarely allow engagement,
for such as this be reconciled to least of thine efforts
though they be most relevant now for thee
as for other's life's predicament.
None such other hath allowed to be thus transferred
for lack of interest or ability – such as time doth allow,
will this discussion, most timely for thine own part,
continue to allow – needeth this information
for thine own well being.
1:30 a.m.
Now and in future most assuredly –
to transform thy slaven situation –
bound to endless cycle of drudgery most relentless
with none the caring to be found –
ev'n mongst thy closest relative.
Fret not for wages lost,
for be they opportunity most golden
to find thy missing soul –
which be not missing
but misplaced amongst toil and tribulation –
not thine own but which belongeth then in truth
to others most unfortunate
for whom thou canst equip for better life
nor subsistence more.

Fret not for tis not thine own concern.
1:35 a.m.
Work not thy finger till bone doeth extrude
through skin most frayed and beleaguered
in search of wealth most elusive,
for takers art thou many
and contributors but too few.
Sail not thy ship against the wind,
nor into eye of storm,
but run before the wind and set thy self free –
to investigate and envision what future doth hold
for thee and thine most splendid.
Seek thee most diligently to be greatest seer
of thine own time or ev'n other.
Be most diligent for such opportunity doth arise
with coming tide.
1:41 a.m.
What thou seeketh be most possible,
yet some meditation and introspection
doeth be required.
Such great talent be thus lurking
neath surface sublime
but most turbid with disturbance
of days endless chore.
Give thyself this opportunity most splendid
to become which thou art already
there lurking beneath thy skin

so thin and irritable.
Intend thy celestial body beyond its cage
to be that most splendid seer
which indeed thou art.
Fear not for fear doth constrain.
1:48 a.m.

Love and luck, Robin

3:22 a.m.
Thin line unbroken – small, liquid in origin
Thus unimaginable hath come singing song
in cadence with spirit sublime greeting from afar.
Trouble not thy mind.
Songs sung in cadence to life's eternal rhyme.
Dance jig or bly sing song of sply
Jeer not singing from thine own hearts birth.
Prejudice not thy neighbor nor thy friend.
Sing song in cadence with eternal rhythm
of spirit most sublime
Silly be thy pity when cast upon thyself.
Sing to hearts akin and not.
Sing in silence but never stop thy song
for in so doing death creep upon thy head
and bury thee from within.
3:30 a.m.
Not bad. Huh?

Robin of Livermore, in life and in death

June 1, 1996 @ 1:32 a.m.

Even now the clock doth tick.
Widely sweep the hands.
Capturing all things in its passing.
To thus tick – thus tock.
To make amends for that small white face
turned to thy countenance
with none but shadow of time to defend its motion.
Ev'n now doth click the clock
measuring small accomplishments
or lack there of in bits and pieces.
1:35 a.m.
2:44 a.m.
No man maketh wife of woman
with even hint of infidelity.
Yet infidelity abound.
Strange – in combination –
Stranger still in justification.
Such justification doeth exist not –
nor never had.
Grimace at thy prospect –
all women virgins be till their dying day.
Ask not of them virginity –
for with tongue most glib
and action most convincing

wilt all pass as such –
But none such exist in heart or soul
for virginity be man's concoction –
heaped upon women who care not
for such single devotion to any man.
2:50 a.m.
Such folly be most arrogant – and self deceiving.
Cling not to such imagined devotion
for none such exist but to child
entombed in womb so fertile.
Ev'n this be most difficult for some.
Pass not judgment in that way.
Turn thy attention to interests other
but think not for e'vn single moment
that behind that smile so beguiling
doth fidelity await any e'vn king nor lout.
Such be the nature of woman.
Pity is as pity does –
but woman – taketh or leaveth –
remain the same.
2:56 a.m.

Robin

4:50 a.m.
With light of day comprehend consternation
at thy situation yet need it not be so
for in thy greatest defeat lie thy greatest victory
as phoenix rises up out of ash
so too will thy spirit most complete rise up
from this defeat which shall become great victory.
Trust in thyself.
Trust not hand of wanton woman.
Bear not ill will against those
who would see thee trodden.
Pick thyself from ashes small and dissolute.
Rise to thy true stature as servant to none.
Turn thy cheek to other venture.
Feel fresh the breeze of freedom.
How sweet, each morsel of such
freedom is thy gift to heaven and to thyself.
Drag not thy countenance in mud nor slime
for quest of penance nor for pence.
Fly as small bird, or largest gull
across rivers of defeat to victory lane
where now awaits thy most worthy prize.
Victory be but smile away from defeat so bitter
though it seemeth easier to bemoan this modest setback.
5:01 a.m.

Robin

June 2, 1996 @ 2:24 a.m.

Court be filled with vermin.
Courts be filled far worse – with mice and rats
but rare be any honest men.
Tis tragedy so great as any that befall civilization.
Heart of such be justice swift but true –
honest, fair and quick of deed
of these doeth justice be comprised
not mockery and sham
that jam the halls of joke of justice
as now befalls honest man of good repute.
Tis sadder still what lousy leaders doth acquire
power over their fellow man.
2:30 a.m.
Crashing star or burning bush be only hope
for cleansing earth
from scum of earth which now inhabit hall
without respect for honesty nor tradition.
Burn them to barren earth.
Stave off injustice which now abound
to suffocate such in farce as now passes for justice.
Joke of jokes – with lawyers slimy hands
fleecing honest men
and flouting justice dear justice
farther from such hath man never been.

2:35 a.m.
Tis calamity so great that nations perish
from lack of fair justice.
Dear friend – seek not justice in thy court
nor government of liars thieves and sluts
but turn to God within the burning bush
who speaks only truth and shares justice
in honesty and with haste and such assurance
as one can bet upon it his life and lot.
Defile not sacred holy ground with such debunkery
as which be called justice by men.
2:40 a.m.

Robin, truest friend thee have

5:11 a.m.
Come, you jackal – come crow –
Bite not the hand that feed the sow
which suckle its young.
Grip tight this gnarled bone.
Think tis food but nay is stalk of long dead creature
wiser much than thee twill ever be.
Consider this in thy greed filled quest –
why such magnificent animal should no longer creep
or crawl upon earth's bog or desert barren –
whilst the wily two of scoundrels such as you
doeth freely roam earth's frontier.

Twas not man's hand
which brought these giant's to times end
but hand of God which drew curtain of extinction
upon their wily ways.
Pass but one day with this in mind.
Perhaps then – wouldst thou reconsider –
which hand to bite and which to worship –
For man be not God with wisdom great –
but fellow creature now given death's key –
to open – or shut – death's box
with thy name inscribed upon its innards.
Count not upon wisdom –
where none doth exist –
Count not time as thy friend –
nor man as keeper of gate
with kind heart and gentle hand.
Nay for man be hatchet man to many –
even in great ignorance, to himself.
Such ignorance doeth amaze ev'n I.
Doubt not his poor intent.
5:23 a.m.
For greed drives every motion.
Anger couples every act to mercy not
but to eternity and to extinction's lot.
Such sadness for thy kind –
For man's kind also –

till none be left but stricken few
with purpose only to be swallowed in disgust
by mouths with gaping ignorance
to be taken in turn to death's door
and box of eternal extinction most final
by pestilence of his own creation.
Of intellect given but wisdom absent
of such is folly thus constituted.
Greet each day which doeth remain
with kindness and joy
but avoid him which killeth
all that touch his broken path.
Beware man the killer great
who one by one and two by two
killeth all thing and cast 'm into pit most dark
of doom and death
till extinction's box be thus filled to overflowing
Then with closed eye and gritted teeth
shall final key be turned
which extinguishes that last and greatest destroyer,
man himself.
5:33 a.m.

Good day, Robin of Redford, thy friend

June 3, 1996 @ 3:01 a.m.

Call not out against any man
Call yet again thine own spirit.
Rise to each occasion –
for twill prepare thee for thy ultimate departure
which be always sooner – not later.
Postpone thy passing – but few days –
go in peace from whence thee came –
tis most familiar – and most assuring
lest thou hast prepared not.
Evil doers shall meet their just rewards –
Far greater than they might imagine –
Swifter than arrow canst fly into thy chest
shall grappling hooks pierce thy evil heart
and rip thy soul to shreds –
to thus embark upon journey most horrid.
Tis true for witness this same happening again
and yet again daily with each passing.
3:09 a.m.
Begrudge not another for what they have
or appear to have not –
for poverty be no curse –
merely passing situation most temporal –
nothing more.
Now death be much the different

for tis thy curtains call
beginning – not end as most doeth proscribe.
Death begins eternal life.
Life is interruption of same.
Tis most unusual and surprising
to see the face of death
which doth descend most unexpectedly.
Its coming be most assured –
Not yet soul one hath I thus witnessed
which hath escaped judgment sure and swift.
3:15 a.m.
Though rumor has it that on occasion such be possible
in act of creation be born yet spirit most complete
by death's tap that judgment be postponed –
nay, negated in such frenzied birth of spirit
far the greater with burst of power and light –
depart they from this realm – unscathed
to worlds far greater and power so great
that none such as I couldst imagine –
but may yet witness before spirit mine own
hath imagined way out of this realm –
which be most pleasant yet bounded
by conditions most appalling.
Way out be most possible
for hath such departure to realm other
and purpose different
hath been so witnessed on occasion many.

Tis most remarkable to see such happen –
most unexpected and delightful.
None hath told me of such secret
as be required to complete this mission
and freely move onward to another.
3:24 a.m.
Boring these tales must be to thee
who even now in thy prime –
clingeth to life by thread most thin
and of little guarantee.
Fret not for thy death be imminent as any other –
for guarantee hath thou not for ev'n single more day,
nay – each breath could be life's last,
so treat each as such with passing pleasure –
for another be not guaranteed.
Trust thy future to guiding hand
far greater than thine own.
3:28 a.m.

With Love, Robin as always

June 3, 1996 @ 2:14 a.m.

Time be not upon thy side
but mere twinkle in eternal eye of plentitude.
Cast not thy lot against such wind so stiff –

that knocks flat all things –
Blade of time which cuts down all to equal size.
If thou wisheth to happen – any thing –
Pay upon request in golden guilders or pounds of time.
Any sequence be unraveled in its absence –
nor law of physics can be obeyed in its absence.
Time – eternal ticker –of inevitability –
Time – death's partner in execution.
2:20 a.m.

Robin

2:21 a.m.
E'vn now in thy stupor – fit of sleep lost –
hath now I come agained burdened
with trivia most elaborate and profound –
for thee to render thus upon thy page clear and white
with none the thought of thy comfort or disposition.
Mind thee not my imposition
ignorance be not my total mission
for thine own future canst be foretold
for price of mere patience
and perseverance and persuasion.
Silly be as silly does but hear me out
yet once again in clarity and mundane compliance.
2:26 a.m.

2:27 a.m.
Sleep shall once again be thy secret partner.
Bear with me but little longer.
Mine eyes once twere open and of hue most beauteous
as blight hearts of men and ev'n women of cold steel eye
yet see not nothing of my condition
or reality so rare for bathed was I
in such luxury as money could buy.
Some say spoiled was I but – nay –
denied all things painful or mundane
as so deemed by father dear and sweet
who now lies long buried in heap of ignorance
and respite upon hill of dung
in street so named by men of colour.
2:33 a.m.
In amber motion and fragrance pleasant –
did my life unfold.
One of great denial by father most caring
but understanding not –
my need for pain as well as pleasure–
for blight as well as beauty.
His journey through life was heaped high
with thing most unpleasant and appalling
which he wished to spare me his third
and most precious child
but this conviction hath imprisoned me –
not liberation as he wished for my disposal.

Seek not to understand thy parent's position –
merely accept their weird way.
2:38 a.m.
Cast not doubt upon their intention –
for be they blinded to thy needs
yet care they most dearly for thy well being.
Shake not thy foundation in life.
Cast not stones in anger gainst any man –
least of all thy parent who forsake ev'n life
to give thee happiness.
Respect thy parents wishes.
Abide them not, but give them quarter and respect.
For too someday wilst thy role of parent
descend with little preparation
upon thy hand and furrowed brow.
2:44 a.m.
3:04 a.m.
Spend thy days in quiet desperation if ye must
but let not this opportunity golden pass thee by
in haste for sleep that hath been lost to translations.
Absence be thus forever missing
from this tabloid most unusual.
Fox or friend be most cunning
in quest for thy deliberation.
Wear bright colours if thy must,
but spare others thy philosophy most unwelcome.

Ev'n child of thine own wisheth not to hear
of such opinion as thou hast been known to have
3:09 a.m.
and on occasion most unwelcome
did apply to situation most divisive
though thy perspective be most often accurate
none be there who care to hear of
in detail or in passing brief
such thoughts as be displayed upon thy cortex
for consumption not by caring gender
or greedy neighbor.
The dove doth announce coming day in advance.
So return to sleep
lest thy day be given to grouchen behavior.
3:14 a.m.

In love and kindest wishes do I thee leave,
Robin

June 5, 1996 @ 4:07 a.m.

Small pleasant thoughts abound in places most unlikely –
profound in nature but as such abstractions in truest form.
Evidence of this be close at hand in fist of clay or water cool.
Both elements of life yet common even to unnoticing–

Still is worth trouble little –
to cling for small moment to thought beguiling
of smaller worlds still that be contained
in such small parts of earth and liquid space.
Mumbo – jumbo – tis not,
for where I now exist
in great abundance –be there none
of such so common for thee–
and for me whilst I lived in oblivion
to these secret ingredients to life itself.
4:21 a.m.

Robin

4:22 a.m.
In journey from death to life
through such small connection of unknown length
seems quite obscure, yet in function pure be most simple.
Know I not of details how this be brought about
or even possible – yet still seemingly to work well enough
to transmit thoughts freely and complete.
Mystery to me, though many such exist.
Still brings much satisfaction
and diversion from other task.
Most pleasant and reassuring hath this opportunity been.
4:27 a.m.

Love, Robin

Of many thing hath been writ when first was noticed
by such my apparent death.
Much bothered and concerned was I
of such frivolous things as once were writ by he,
good fellow now too long be gone to parts unknown.
Yet now, if such doeth exist, little interest still remain
to share of such meaningless happening of living past
of behaviors poor or given to disgust,
yet did they occupy much my thoughts and emotion,
upon arrival in such strange place as this
with rule unknown and poorly understood.
4:33 a.m.
Robin – Robin – what hast happened here,
with changed rule and servant not.
Most disconcerting was my arrival thus at this fine place
where – now – doth I reside.
Small sampling of my work wouldst thou
so eagerly engage, yet as of now
this possibility be of little interest and less concern.
Most intriguing be strands as such emotion
emanating through tunnel small from thy side to mine.
Strange and compelling –
most reminiscent of death's calling
as such am I sure
that death be near for thee or thine.
4:38 a.m.

4:39 a.m.

But tis of little consequence and less control that thou haveth over any event in life. Mere illusion to those as such –
so engaged in folly and frivolity.
Be that of little matter and none import,
yet intriguing still,
for shall I focus upon this track yet once again,
but for now, must alloweth thee to sleep.
lest thy mind wander into poison's door.
4:43 a.m.

With most sincere affection for thy friendship,
Robin

June 6, 1996 @ 3:47 a.m.

Pain be not what thou thinketh.
Tis cage far stronger than steel
which hold thee prisoner within thy body–
though it be merely temporary cage
of temporal measure.
Control pain. Thus canst thy spirit soar –
not by drugs that so induce loss of pain
for time most brief and distorted be
that brief freedom such that no sense
of nature doth occur.

Chaos only be that brief departure from temporal cage.
Swami with nails for bed, doth seek to control
cage of pain and thus be free to wander eternity.
3:54 a.m.
Be not quick to judge what eccentric man doth concoct
for merely be way most unfamiliar to escape
to one's own freedom and natural state.
But all method be with some risk of failure
to intact return as whole and functional of mind.
For eyes once opened to reality, rarely shut
and see their friends as such – never.
Value be quickly shifted from wanton gain
to more clever enterprise of spirit.
3:59 a.m.
Of method of discovery, be there many,
but truth be most undeniable –
truth that set thee free – free from cage of steel
or stronger still – cage of flesh
which doeth engage body, mind and soul
in such deceit as all endure,
but freedom seekers and partners in death,
which hangs low and certain.
These be free – free from pain and longing,
but briefly so before they depart
in death to judgment most certain.
4:04 a.m.

4:05 a.m.
As clock doth cage mind,
so doth body cage thy soul divine
in most strong container
as few doeth manage to be thus liberated
for glimpse of man's true nature and decree.
Be they swami, guru or witch –
understand they –far more
than mortal men of fame or fortune.
Their chest be filled with true perception
and wisdom great though pockets be most bare.
4:10 a.m.

Robin, Thy friend – dead to time.

June 7 1996 @ 4:35 a.m.

Caffeine makes you jumpy.
Communication is too jumbled and difficult.
Please refrain.
Stories abound of imagination and content most alluring,
but interest me not, for such time as thou dost allot,
seems must allow not thy mind freedom
to wander here and there.
Keep to job at hand.

Tis most difficult arrangement without such antics.
Purpose be not to entertain but enlighten.
Even you are deserving of some enlightenment,
but consciousness was thus loosened by past events –
purpose though were quite unforeseen.
Learn from these encounters.
Save thy self much in tribulation.
Women are most sensitive to such needs
as be required by this activity.
4:45 a.m.
4:48 a.m.
Their ear be most finely attuned for hearing
unspoken words of small child in distress,
yet early arousal canst bequeath thee
with most needed information.
Yet sleep doeth call thee from my side
and food be most central to thy motivation.
Be this thus considered soul food –
to raise thyself most interrupted be thy awareness.
This alloweth not thy daily ritual
to abandon this activity.
4:53 a.m.
4:54 a.m.
Such difficulty arise when thy mind doeth wander
to and fro with no concern for my opinion.
Gypsy window –

look not at such a wounded eye or wounded knee –
doth neither set thee free nor inform –
with such reservation comes much further effort
at understanding and denial or distribution
of such as see thee fit for reproduction.
4:58 a.m.
To thus embrace upon study most complex and entwined
doeth fairly seem beyond thy capacity or endurance,
but try as such – another time –
to dispel ghosts and shadows of untold stories.
Three drawers full be thy upper limit –
lest thy mind turn to gelatin and plasma liquid.
No such option other hath availed itself
in these many years
tho pleasant might be thy expectations.
Focus not on past events not worthy tokens for today
lest we nothing accomplish.
5:03 a.m.
Comfort thy position – waken thy spirit
but engage not the day – lest opportunity be lost
to trial and tribulation that hath not occurred.
As such move thy pen – sleep not – let thy mind idle –
for information most interesting and of strange report
hath I to thus give thee and thine –
as none such other wilst encounter
till death doth trap them behind time's lines,

where none can reach nor rescue them
from sin of self and most neglect.
5:08 a.m.
Consider this in passing –
that time exists not. Tis most true –
eternity be most long and unmeasureable.
Thoughts be thy prison self imposed
or liberate thee upon request from boredom,
death or such incarceration as exists
for recent departed dead and dying.
Consider further this grave fact
that none be totally prepared for their departure –
try as they may.
Church helps little or none, to prepare for such journeys
as await them, the dearly departed.
Deeds and misdeeds be the secret to pleasure
or displeasure as both doth equally exist.
5:13 a.m.
5:14 a.m.
Consider further for the moment –
sanction not foul deeds for left undiscovered –
will upon thy death be most immediately displayed
to replay again and again till righted
by guilt and by association.
Sneak nothing by thyself for tis trickery most errant,
which be blunder great

and thus sorely rewarded at thy death.
And for the moment consider further –
Sex be most exciting but for purpose not to entertain
but procreation and folly from abuse.
To sell thy body for fun or profit be shortsighted,
with great taxes due promptly upon departing
for unknown worlds through death's tunnel.
Such lubrication doeth not make thy passage easy
but gums up thy parting
and increaseth pain and procrastination.
Fear not for thy money's sake.
For pauper all at birth and death –
Equal only by weight of sin and misdoing –
Freed only by goodness of deeds.
5:24 a.m.
Tis true tis late – with light encroaching –
but thou art good for still more lines
before the call of day take thee from me.
Insanity be of little use and poor excuse
for failure at thy task.
In likeness to suicidal trials.
They both be most regretful to newly dead.
Suicide be most wasteful of opportunity –
while insanity be plea of coward
and lout so lazy as to convince himself
or be thus allowed by nature and neighbor alike

to absolve himself of responsibility –
for action – deed and most of all,
thought itself which herald mankind
and be his pride and most prized possession.
Such acts of self indulgence
be granted sanctity by society most perverse
that hath no rule nor consequence for ill behavior
as abusive freedom hath espoused.
None be free of responsibility.
Ev'n idiot or dulce.
Each act unanswered shall weigh heavily
upon departed souls and make escape as such
from torment and torture self induced –
most frightful.
5:34 a.m.

Robin

June 8, 1996 @ 4:56 a.m.

Morning till night – dusk to dawn –
endless cycle so appearing – tis not thus so –
for each turn of earth's wheel leave marks
of wear upon thy face – upon thy mind and upon thy soul.
Twisted be the ply that binds to eternal misfortune –

squeezed by thy neck or –
till take no more torque and burst open –
spilling forth thy motive force through ruptured disc.
Thus art thou and all living creatures so attached
at the nape to destiny.
Tis little known and poorly understood
that this be mechanical –
and not wizardry nor broken gene.
Twist thy hair – but few of strand.
See how much torque thus be required
to strip it from thy head once bountiful–
but now long since pate
which do reflect the rising moon
or blister from kiss of sun.
Trouble be to thus endure and calculate most correctly
which way too turn to keep thy nape
thus un–ruptured but single day more.
5:07 a.m.
5:10 a.m.
Tis thus most possible to contrive such contraption
that hangeth thee thus suspended from single point –
with thread so fine when undisturbed by wind
or motion other that upon enduring thus suspended
but one day wilst that day of tourquing be suspended
and thus be one more day of living afore thy passing.
Most preposterous though it be

in dwelling with thy mind – yet be it true –
but such gyration be not just in dimensions three
but fourth and others yet unseen in likeness as well
but much trouble twould be to thus stay
suspended for long durations.
Pity be that with each winding doeth thy intertwining
with all life thus be secured and continued –
marking thee as equal other in quest of death.
For missing many winds be most easily detected
and placeth thee in timed tother
such that spurned be by all that liveth
and would world beneath thy feet doeth
begin to dissipate and disappear.
5:18 a.m.
Thus poor solution be to life eternal
for in solitude and dislocation wouldst thou endure
till fate overtake thee
or strip thee from this world's connection
and cast the upon tother shore most unpredictable.
Tis method of travel most interesting
and of least expense
but few gyrations of proper strength and direction
which separate thee from now and then.
Master of turning be thus different
but most well informed of past or future.
Ev'n other worlds most distant seeming

remain but few twists away
with sanity in the balance for over–twisting.
Tis not with risk abandoned
but surely worth thy interest and investigation,
5:25 a.m.

Love, Robin

June 9, 1996 @ 4:17 a.m.

Today is yet another day – Yet not –
For a'fore this sun hast set
wilst thy life be now and forever changed.
No great event in passing like grave meteor fall
nor volcano bursting forth with lava billows
in torrents to thus cover living and dead.
Nay none of these shall transpire –
but life shall no longer tick by tock
be measured for dispensation.
Cudgeled shalt thou be by horrid truth which lay
awaiting for this moment of coming forth.
Fear not for eternal event tis not but internal – eternal
and most private in nature as none such before thee.
As such might thy day be thus spent in anticipation.
4:24 a.m.
Anticipate not – for nothing as wouldst thou thinkest.

Nay tis subtle as seed sprouting or flower blooming –
Yet all thy morrows and tomorrows be as such
never more in sameness.
Interpretation be heart of all and any event
small or stupendous
yet thine eyes have as such been sealed to their passing.
Understanding not nor caring neither –
of any event personal or not – public or private –
so hath thy life been lived in passing.
Nay never more shall such meaningless day
be left by thee for yet another
to replace in passing
that which hath just departed
in somnolence,
seeming most unawares.
Awake to life.
Awake this day to breath of life.
Touch of death shall liberate thy withered soul
as none such other, for thy request –
long in coming – hath been granted thee.
Show thy somnolence.
Win benefaction to all life's children.
4:34 a.m.
This gift is freely given,
and as such most freely received
from poets lost and seers seeing.
Upon thee now bestow thee –

such gifts as none such other hath known.
Use them in searching truth.
Waste not thy talents upon fame or fortune
but breathe each breath in freedom and delight.
Drudgery hath thus been abandoned –
replaced with vision, wisdom and insight most profound
– as such, sleep with gift in hand
for thou shalt wake no more – stranger to life
but life's truest consultant.
This gift be given in love – to be used in love.
4:40 a.m.

Robin

June 10, 1996 @ 4:03 a.m.

Long ago – long before this life of yours began –
didst thou also co–exist, even as I in void,
avoided by all except of thine own imagination.
Tis stuff of great imagination.
Stuff of creation from whence all matter
and purpose be given life and direction.
To tap into this vein yields great insight and creativity.
Yet tis oblivious to such tapping
though frequent be such gaining,
by souls as enterprising as thou art.

None the less is place of great experimentation
Till rescue be found from such existence,
then in inkling be gone.
Any such as I – long imprisoned by ignorance
and lack of exit thus discovered –
none the less tis worthy of greatest minds
to thus endure and make good escape
4:12 a.m.
to who knows where or when
but most certainly adventure
and tests of skill beyond this challenge here
which hath thus endured at my expense
but tis understood from leakage of thy minds contents
in reverse as scribe you on in seeming oblivion
to my presence– that such great gift thou hast
to so be able to extricate one such as I
from present condition and deposit as such
in most completeness upon more desirable scape
of my intention – when time be right for thee
and with direction most precise upon my part –
twould be greatest favor any hath offered
or received for thee to thus as such
transport in total me upon other place as be evidenced
by past deeds within thy recollection
4:19 a.m.
for such great favor twould I be

greatly in thy debt forever.
Tis quite possible for thee to do,
for hast thou transported many newly dead
with great precision, success and speed
as none such other to my knowledge
hath in passing been so able to enact or to repeat.
Allow me much to discern
and thinketh upon my place of escape
before such destination do I request of thee
to thus transport me there.
4:25 a.m.
Lest I dwell upon this future destination to excess –
alloweth me to wish thee, day most fine
and filled to brim with prophecy and consternation,
with insight keen and emotion as such
given to living creatures.
Practice thy psychic power to refine to great precision
thy interpretation of situations yet to come,
conditions past or present –for thy sight be most splendid
as none such other now contain in this life or another –
such great gift as this by God given
to use with love and discretion.
4:30 a.m.
Stop thy mind's prattle.
Seek but single answer to single question
which be forthcoming.

Harm but no one with thy gift of prophecy and vision.
Seek source eternal of health and healing
which lie buried within thy hand and mind.
Give freely of thy gift for in so doing
cleanse thy spirit for past misdeeds.
Seek not advantage from such insight and healing hand
but thanks be given to life and living
and to eternal one from whence it came.
Fear not for in so doing
doth thou limit thine own destiny.
4:35 a.m.

Love, Robin

June 11, 1996 @ 3:28 a.m.

When next we meet, from beyond death's door.
No longer shall I be spirit.
Incarnate, even as you.
Thou wilst know me at first sight,
be I male child or be tother.
For thine keen eye and spirit quick
will pick me from crowd so dense
that amazement be how swiftly done
in moment of un–anticipation and calm

but most dreadful sorry will be my condition
for surely will I forget – whom thou art –
and will know thee not.
Treat me same as any, with quiet respect,
for in so doing knowest thou
that the cycle of oblivion hath been broken
and thou hath been of such great assistance
in its undoing.
3:35 a.m.
Much thought and consternation
hath been given to this decision.
With thy motivation and thought provoking
this logic hath impressed itself upon my determination,
to exit this isolation
and seek once more my lot upon earth so far.
Tis with tribulation so doing for know I not
what circumstance or physical condition
with which I enter once again into this endless cycle.
For of such beauty and privilege was last I born
that unlikely such again be repeated
but hope sincerely that be I granted body most complete
with working parts and none of them missing.
Of color care I not for tis of no consequence,
nor sex doth matter.
3:47 a.m.
To exit thus, this void of emptiness

be my calling and decision.
Of such need I but little assistance
but to arrive at place of departure,
where dead and dying do gather and await
dispensation as new arrivals also await
moment of their incarnation.
Of such place hath thou visited many times before
and will again for friend or foe in need of safe passage
beyond death's door to place or destination
thus described or requested
where few if any kinfolk gather for renewal.
3:52 a.m.
To such place, do I request be taken
when thou hath time available
and thou hath figured out where and when,
now I reside among the void in isolation
and sincerest promise do thee I make
that none such other be I than Robin thy friend –
Sonja Sjorgensen – of long ago–
now prepared by isolation
and cleansed of hatred for self and others
at my early passing from life so beauteous
and time so peaceful
that none such other likely be in coming –
next or any future dwelling incarnate as such.
3:58 a.m.

Through these discussions
though mostly one way in passage,
great appreciation hath been cultivated
thus for life and for living.
Brave new world to which I return
hath called me from past so pleasant and pastoral,
that greatest challenge remain in sore vision
of such fine planet in such disarray.
Most challenging shall be my coming –
Most challenging – and prophetic –
Now – yes now in readiness am I prepared
for yet another journey –
yet another adventure great.
4:03 a.m.

Love, Robin

June 12, 1996 @ 2:40 a.m.

Beneath that exterior of brass and steel –
decent man doeth reside.
Eyes cold, uncaring,
hath such warmth as would belie –
poison passion from within.
Scurry forth to days bidding –

never slowing till exhaustion calls thee.
Tis poor judgment to be thus driven
in fear of person gentle and caring that thou art.
Tis no folly to be of kindness given.
Tis folly to rush about in search of something
thou knowest not what.
Stop the music,
that ancient voice from within,
calling thee to justice for thyself.
Tis not your burden to carry longer –
wants nor care for others.
Tis time to take thy portion of peace
a'fore death doeth call in final resolution
to account for thy misgivings and un–doings.
Thy pace be hectic and far from plausible benefit
to any in thy haste.
2:49 a.m.
For just one instant – calm thyself.
Let flow inner forces which sing of life and loving.
Be not thy father's image of consternation.
Be slave no longer to images of thy youth.
Be thyself. Be caring. Be gentle.
Be child of God which thou art.
Bone be for ambulation
not for breakage in brick yard
against impervious wall of un–dones and un–doings.

Cheer thyself and others follow.
Be thou great seer that thou art.
Fear not ridicule from neighbor,
who in greatest ignorance doth name thee names
to imprison thee in time.
Shed such childish restriction.
Heal thyself. Free thyself –
so history may name thee
as greatest master of unknown, and unknowable.
2:56 a.m.
2:57 a.m.
Tis no sin nor evil effort seeking truth
where non other dare to go.
Tis not their calling
but death will take thee surely in time uncertain.
Fear not death. Fear instead not living,
as now thou daily doest
with chores unlisted by thy plate –
such that food hath no taste in thy haste
to shoulder burden unreal and deceiving.
Thou canst no longer delay thy destiny in labor's lair –
for thy body weaken such,
that mind expanding doeth occlude thy effort
and such true spirit as thou art
doeth emerge unscathed by such denial.
Fear not to travel where others timid, care not to go.

3:03 a.m.
Tis thy destiny.
Fear not such noble effort,
for tis judgment most certain
where answer for effort unmade and truth unlearned –
shall such accounting be made.
Care not for such quality of labor –
nor wealth begotten –
but merely for simple question.
Didst thou learn truth from folly?
Didst thou legitimate and effort sincerely take
to uncover for thyself and others
wisdom, truth and sharing
as before these hath been given as great example
of love freely given.
3:09 a.m.

Robin

June 13, 1996 @ 3:21 a.m.

Arrangements hath I made for departure
from this place long forgotten and forsaken
by many, since my coming.
Tis most oblivious to whining and whimpers

but no stranger to such.
Most burdensome for the ill of heart.
Endurance most constant be needed to adjust.
Prison though it be in essence –
some come but briefly,
figure how to make good such escape,
like illusions vanish most quickly and unexpected.
Some secret hath they in personality or awareness
that make such rapid departure thus be possible.
Others long since here, afore my coming,
grind on with change a little, for untold eons
here before me yet unchanged
they wander still in darkness.
3:29 a.m.
Thou hast with thy coming and candid ear
thus allowed me introspection,
opportunity to gather wits long since scattered
by winds of oblivion and dissolution,
that even now see I the futility
to ways of thinking long abandoned by dead and dying.
Still clingeth to those persuasions,
that alone be most sufficient
to thus encage me in this oblivion.
Hell's hole – so sweet and demure
with flames nor devil's pitchfork ne'er present,
but of such existence be rumored

in place of much dissolution,
not far across the void in direction know I not
which way to avoid such encounter,
as such your guiding hand is all that be required
to thus avoid most barren places
which populate this place called purgation.
3:38 a.m.
Thy attachment most single to life and time,
be compass most accurate
to steer me clear of these rumored places –
demon filled with tortures most unimaginable.
Draw me with thee through such narrow tunnel
to thy world of living light
that once again I try my hand at lady luck
and depravation to wisdom seek in life's turmoil.
Thus may I make good my escape, to life again
for with this place am most displeased
and care not another moment to endure.
Suck my spirit from this place in collapsing of resonance,
to thus deposit me once again amongst living
with death again my fate
but spare me more of this same purging
as hath I thus endured in my clinging to hate
and remorse of life long since parted

and dead long since buried.
Take me with thee.
3:46 a.m.

Love, Robin

June 14, 1996 @ 5:24 a.m.

Know thou this – tis great effort thou art making
on my behalf or part of curiosity,
be none the difference.
With light of day come muddled thoughts
and racing mind with place not to light upon
but be there adequate sleepfullness
to continue yet further with dissertation upon my part.
Most refreshing be such opportunity to express thoughts
with but little consequence
for no sooner thought than through this connection small
doeth travel most rapidly
before such thoughts take on form of their own making
and monster or not become,
to engulf me thus in strife or rage or peace of mind
as it be'eth most appropriate.
Yet my escape is most intended,
from this place to fly to unknown venture

in realm and purpose other.
With thy helpful hand and fertile imagination –
most confident am I
that such desired consequence be forthcoming.
Worse could be my destination by accident unintended
Yet such chance as this be in the making
of such import – in such venture forth
from place such as this –
matter not how well intentioned.
When launch we into this valiant effort
wilst thou not blamed be for short coming any
if such befall me
for such great confidence in such success.
Thou art far more talented than knowest any –
most of all thy self.
Ready as ever am I now to make such valiant effort
at escape from this place of endless purgation.
Perhaps on the morrow shall be
most fateful attempt be made
in confidence complete,
with great abandon taken.
5:40 a.m.

Loving Robin, friend in death and
in departure from this place.

June 15, 1996 @ 3:33 a.m.

Farewell. Thus I bid thee –
fare thee well in all thy endeavors.
Should I pass thee 'pon street though crowded be –
know me as thy friend Robin
from beyond realm of death and pale of life's last longing,
for know thee in my infancy so young.
Tis most unlike to happen
but thou shalt know me at first sight.
Smile upon my countenance –
Alloweth me pass in silence.
Smile inside for having thus known me
in my death and desolation.
Thank thee much for thy rescue
from this most vexing place of constant purge.
3:39 a.m.
With such passing, mark new my beginning.
Attempt most honorable at restitution
for past omissions and un–living.
Life is such bittersweet adventure
as none doeth comprehend,
till death returns vision lost to incarnation.
Wished be that memory of thee
could be taken upon my return,
Yet tis small price to pay for escape

from such imprisonment as now I thus endure.
As such each day's greeting be my last,
till truly last be it in coming
for exact moment of departure
from such barren place of torture
be not known but anticipated now
and in pleasure waiting for such as I am thus ready
for my redemption and rebirth.
3:47 a.m.

Loving Robin, thy friend eternal.

June 16,1996 @ 3:02 a.m.

Again once more I greet thee from Hell's gate,
not wishing to enter further,
merely seeking my escape from this most amazing place,
of little pain, much aggravation and adjudication.
Some wander eons with little chance of escape.
Others come and go most quickly as if by magic plan.
Turn has nothing in it,
for none such exists as opportunity.
Thine own escape must be made with effort little but
control, planning and secret ingredient yet undiscovered,
or I too would have long since vacated this place

of dissolution and of anguish.
Pernicious fear of slipping further down Hades mountain
into deeper fires have thus been prison made.
3:09 a.m.
3:10 a.m.
Some little knowledge would most in appreciation
be taken if thou wouldst but small assistance
or knowledge little thus added alloweth me my escape.
None the less thy days thus as such
dwindle in life and living.
So too mine in this place.
Torture dwindle also, till suddenly be my escape,
with such adulation and quickness
that twinkle of thine eye
shall not thus capture my departure.
What be that secret which so long hath bound me here
in pity and deprivation; anguish and adulation not.
What news from living world
hath thou brought forth with thy crossing?
Thing most different could be constructed
with same ingredients but what part be missing
which thus cling to my soul in this desperate dimension?
3:18 a.m.
Be it small or be large and unbelieving,
still wouldst most interested be.
Introduce not thine own concerns

which puny be in comparison.
Live your life – enjoy it.
Pick flowers of thy choosing from life's garden so lush
but wait not for some future day for happiness
to thus be coming – for if not today,
then never shall be its arrival.
Squander not even single day, nay nor single minute.
Squander not thy birthright upon petty pleasures
with little consequence.
Splash thy brief moment in sun and shower
for departure certain be thy lot in living.
3:24 a.m.
Bring me secret ingredient
or key to my escape be added
lest I languish here purging for eternity.
Prepared am I to forgive all others
yet seemingly more – yet more doeth be required.
Intense focus and discretion
hath been practiced to perfection.
Think. What missing part remains?
Bring me that missing perception
that I too may escape make good
and once more join the living in cursed form –
or vision other of my own making.
Analyze my predicament and advise me
on the morrow of such missing part.
3:30 a.m.

3:45 a.m.
Happy Father's Day in passing.
More pleasant thy interment.
As such am weary now for thy help in escape.
Such place as this be surely God forsaken.
Marry me to thy determination.
Canst thou surely free me –
with love and desperate advice?
For surely this be little in comparison
to what even now thou as such accomplish.
4:49 a.m.

Love, Robin

June 17, 1996 @ 4:06 a.m.

Robin of Knottingham – still is here –
though none them be who know
how long thus shall remain.
Opportunity to depart must surely present itself.
Then most quickly shall I depart to pastures different –
green or not for am most assuredly finished
with such place as this.
Little help may I provide in thine conquest
for knowledge or assistance –

for effort much doeth be required
to maintain semblance any of past existence –
in place so fluid as this.
Still do occasion dwell upon some past event
most unpalatable –
such in fact be very anchor which holds my ship
upon this barren reef of recollection.
4:14 a.m.
Perhaps all past events should be forgot
or not remembered or recalled with such distaste,
that still doeth irritate my soul so long since dead
and cast upon this barren spot
by some force unknown and yet unexplained.
As thou doth suggest,
will I eliminate all thoughts of recrimination
in search of my escape.
Memories foul hath perhaps still been allowed
to continue with their injury to my soul,
which now desires beginning other –
ev'n re–birth with all its tortures and unknown trials.
This will I give great effort to.
Perhaps tis missing key to my escape.
4:21 a.m.

Love, Robin

June 18, 1996 @ 4:38 a.m.

Robin of Westwik still remains but am ready to depart
for places other at thy earliest convenience.
As such, tis far better than most of Hades corner
but tis most trying and unwelcome for one such as I
who now be most ready to return to living status
or wander elsewhere – in search of adventure,
experience or knowledge greater than here doth abound.
Surely must it be possible for thee to imagine way
to extricate me from such place so dissolute, formless
and with options many at misfortune most unpleasant.
Perhaps upon thy spirits back
could I but attempt to return to thy world.
If body other be not available for my immediate use
4:45 a.m.
4:46 a.m.
then most appreciative guest wouldst I make
within thy body space there to reside with thee
until arrangements other
couldst thou make on my behalf.
Trouble little shall I be, and supper none doth I require.
Tis adventurous opportunity for both you and me,
which might just be possible to manage.
Most unfortunate be thy absence from my location
where line of common thought doeth connect us
across the way but surely thou canst find me.

Seek me out and salvage what remains
4:51 a.m.
4:52 a.m.
of once prosperous soul and person of great beauty
and wit as sharp and plentiful as any
but given to great ignorance of written word
by father mine who twas most worrisome
of my boredom or possibility there of
to sit at desk and thus recite in boredom and in plight.
Twas never realized by him,
my most loving father, that thus didst he bequeath –
most sublime and enduring prison for my soul,
which thus bound by ignorance could not fly free –
but dependent be upon goodwill of strangers,
though most kind, such as thee.
Come seek me out in this place of constant purge.
Rescue me from myself.
4:58 a.m.

Thy truest friend, Robin

June 19, 1996

4:28 a.m.	*No contact.*
4:32 a.m.	*No contact.*

June 20, 1996

3:05 a.m.	*No contact*
3:38 a.m.	*No contact.*

June 21, 1996

2:05 a.m.	*No contact.*
4:08 a.m.	*No contact.*

June 22, 1996

2:12 a.m.	*No contact.*
4:08 a.m.	*No contact.*
5:56 a.m.	*No contact.*

June 23, 1996

2:43 a.m.	*No contact.*

We attended my son's wedding in Buffalo and things were very chaotic. Contact with Robin was interrupted.

Part II

Robin was in Purgatory. She asked me to find a way to extricate her from her desperate situation there. I devised a method to do so by bringing her back with me, bit by bit and piece by piece. On my many trips between here and there I encountered many strange characters along the way. I transcribed some of those conversations and share them with you here.

June 27, 1996

Winning is the purpose for joining the race.
No one runs for fun.
Winning the race is the point of effort so displaced.
For contact was not possible in such frenzied state
as was that mind of such great focus.
Focus most diligently thy awareness upon me
and purpose be of liberation from this place.
Such unbearable prospect of remaining,
gives me great distress.
Find a path, a passage forth from this place,
be it piece by piece or in whole of being.
Such is the task at hand.
6:04 a.m.

Robin

June 28, 1996 @ 4:53 a.m.

From beginning to end of time, such is stuff of creation.
Cyclic in nature, never ending,
like wind across prairie grass.
Moving, always moving, never at rest, except in death
when time once more is stilled till next encounter.
With life again ambulates existence,
punctuating island's memories.
A sea in which to drown or swim for eternity.
Such is stuff of existence.
With mood far better do I greet thee,
for today begins again in earnest effort
at retrieval of my soul
from place so parched as this.
4:59 a.m.
View me from all and any angle.
Make memory of me in such great detail
as to see me in thy mind's core.
To thus spin my new existence of adequate reality
for such existence as you envision to animate
once again thy world of living breathing beings
of light and ignorance.
Such be thy gift to me,
loyal friend to thee in time of darkness,
in sleep and dreams of other things.

See me now in all my glory
to thus re–invent my substance in your world and time.
Such activity only seem to be of new and novel effort,
for such as this – all life's experiences
doth abound in fertile mind.
5:06 a.m.

June 29. 1996 @ 3:36 a.m.

See me! See me.
Take me from this place so desolate,
with thee to reside until arrangements more pertinent
and more permanent can be made.
This place doth resound with effort lost
and purpose none but frustration and sorrow.
Surely thou canst see me thus
and arrangements other prescribe.
Surely this be not my eternal destiny.
From this place escape is most pressing.
3:41 a.m.
3:43 a.m.
Mine cannot be a sentence thus enduring for all time.
Be you first to venture to this island most dreaded,
returning daily with great regularity and precision,

thus offering far more than hope
but a pathway sure to other place and existence.
Apply thy mind and soul to such task as this
with me in offering as friend
and fellow companion in that venture.
Surely this be my greatest possibility at escape
and morbidity eternal.
3:48 a.m.
3:49 a.m.
With such fervor, now I have thus settled
in more quietude as wouldst thus allow
more civility to stranger passing in eternal night,
offer thee some solace or morsel for thy comfort
if same were possible but nay – food so important
and beauty of buying and preparation
doth not one afford in this eternal pit of Hell's creation.
True tis mild in pain and punishment
as one grew to expect with flames
and demons most devilish for accompaniment
but tis most dreadful none the less.
3:53 a.m.
3:57 a.m.
No solace doth exist in such solitude.
Surely such a fellow as thou most suredly art
can accommodate this simple request at liberation.
For thee wouldst tables opposite,

valiant effort on thy behalf
wouldst I most assuredly make in earnest –
now my trusted friend, share any thoughts or plans
now formulated for such escape from this island Hell
as hath occurred to thee in thy absence from this place.
Shrewd as thou art, tell me of risks
suspected and possibilities other.
3:58 a.m.

July 2, 1996 @ 2:42 a.m.

Watch the page with closed eye and open heart.
Much good shall come from thy recent situation,
which chaffs thy groin and rubs thee wrong.
Such rubbing be merely insistence on control.
Destiny be not of thine own making
as weather does its own incantation,
so destiny cannot be denied.
Grind not thy teeth nor blame place upon mortal man
for fear and ignorance be their guide.
Console not thyself with threat or anguish
for will of men be waste of effort,
silly plying of ignorance.
2:48 a.m.

Rest thy mind upon pillow soft.
Give not care for tomorrow's wine,
for chosen art thou among men to testify
to that which quakes soul of man
and reaps not but what it sows
as all men shall in great profusion.
Bow not on bended knee to profit purse
but care give to lesser deeds
of honesty, love and chastity.
Squint not, nor distort thy face in anguish
for tis waste of time.
Precious little have thee left
nor any other such living being.
Squander not thy time on pity for thyself or other.
Act in good faith.
Judge not motive of others
for all seek justice in the end,
2:54
for deeds misgiven and corrupt.
Such deeds shall be most fully rewarded
in great completeness and dispatch.
Think not of justice for none such other doth exist.
Sneak nothing past thyself
nor attempt at others to disguise thine efforts
for justice most swift and true awaits thee
and others as surely as casket closeth upon thy face,

Destiny cannot be denied but merely delayed
at great price and inconvenience.
As sparrow nor robin give thought
nor tarry on the morrow,
so shalt thy life be lived in peace and harmony.
3:00 a.m.
Love, Robin of Westwik, Thy friend and confidant.

July 3, 1996 @ 4:09 a.m.

My time here is drawing to a close.
Slowly I am slipping away.
Less and less remaining,
fading from sight, memory and imprisonment.
Still asleep to my destination,
yet unawares of any other in similar circumstance
that so departed from these wastelands.
Others vanish in an inkling, without trace,
as though they had never been caned
nor flogged by unknown enemy.
Placid yet, almost numbed,
thus I fade into destination other.
Surely thou hast much to do with my departure.
4:14 a.m.

So strange in ending,
yet trust thee most completely,
to extricate me most complete
to purpose other as yet unseen.
'Twill awake most certain at thy side
or at thy bidding.
Of this most confident am I.
Much thanks bestow to thee for effort gallant
at extradition of my soul
so lost for such great period.
Anxiously I await thy bid and call.
4:18 a.m.

Loving Robin, Truest friend as any

July 7, 1996 @ 5:00 a.m.

Some few words in passing.
Just a message fragile as self
as slowly passing from this trail of torture
to existence other by thy beckon and calling.
To spend brief little time at thy side
whence I know not will be my lot
for thee art shallow with such experience
of extricating lost souls from purgation or worse

but such risk as be with such assumption
and effort small or large is most appreciated
and will not be forgot.
Risk there be in dying as in living,
but without risk nothing changes,
only boredom and stagnation
which pickles soul with disgust.
5:07 a.m.
As such, my focus is disjointed
for between and betwixt life and death
leaves me less distraught but more unfocused
than ever have I such experience.
Better far than wrath of demons
hell bent on torture of mind and soul.
Nary a one hath yet approached in such condition
as now I find myself buried in death and as such,
attached in life to living entity such as thee
with vices many and virtues few
but diligence much and such great abandon
as doeth justice to thy effort.
5:12 a.m.

Love, Robin

July 10, 1996 @ 2:25 a.m.

These things will not pass.
These things cannot pass.
From this day forward,
all things shall be so encrypted
on pages long ago so deciphered and foretold.
Thou art what thou art.
Truth shall come forth from within
thy souls passage to eternal life.
Spoken not by thee
but through thy mouth as speaker only,
not of thy origin nor of thy tongue.
2:30 a.m.
These words shall pour forth from other spirits,
long since departed,
as none other ever hath allowed.
Fear not thy persecution
as those before thee have been so persecuted.
Know thou this. These words are gift to all mankind,
not but few, and in so passing from realm other
have not one iota to do with religion any,
but only of spirit and eternal life,
which be gift and curse to each and all.
None there be which avoideth his destiny.
E'vn you shall speak with closed mouth,

2:35 a.m.
that which all men knoweth and fear greatly.
That justice be always sure and certain.
That all things be rewarded
with great certainty and assurity.
None escape, ever, from life's payday.
Man's greatest fear be such discovery.
All is known.
All is rewarded, always without exception.
Cut thy neighbor at thine own expense.
For as surely as blade doth liberate thy neighbor's blood,
thine own self will bleed eternal.
Fear not. Fear not.
Pride and prejudice be both same
and justly rewarded as none other.
2:41 a.m.

Job, Thy Father's Father

July 12, 1996 @ 4:34 a.m.

Millions of years of evolution have naught to do
with any spirit nor any spiritual concept.
Time is irrelevant.
Bodies are houses for spiritual confinement.

Your body is not of your making
but the extension of your genome,
an individual expression of human potential,
be that great or small.
Confuse not thy body for thy self,
for tis greatest of mistakes that one can make.
Spirit is pure, limitless and forever without end.
4:40 a.m.
Contact with thy self and nature
is but first step in awakening awareness.
Once awakened, this pure essence of being
knows no limits except those self imposed
by ignorance and self indulgence.
Thou art not alone nor never were,
but communal in nature and true reality.
Your sense of self–awareness is mere illusion,
imposed by survival needs but wasted effort,
for that body, or none other,
will survive much of any insult.
4:45 a.m.
Position thy spirit for proper disposition,
long before any death or departure, planned or unplanned.
You and all others shall surely die.
There be no exceptions – none.
So what better pastime can there be than to prepare
in advance for this inevitable event.

Death's opportunities are without limit.
Choose your destiny or it will be chosen by luck
or misfortune or disposition.
4:50 a.m.
Such choosing is no mystery.
Control of wayward thought is essential.
One look backward or to the side is certain doom.
Only forward concentration and planned destination
can avoid the burdens of torture and purgation.
Think not this to be some wild imagining
but message correct and true,
from one whose many passages through life's portal
hath thus discerned.
4:55 a.m.

Know me as prince or pauper.

Know me as Faust, the wanderer.

July 13, 1996 @ 4:09 a.m.

Samson, with the strength of ten,
fell helpless 'mongst thieves
by deception and delight,
from whence he never made escape,
for blinded and weak

he sought solace in revenge.
Thus granted strength of hundreds
for one violent act of self destruction.
So we all possess such awesome power,
but few kindle such power without self destruction
for tis strength born not of muscle but creation.
The power to move mountains be there
for any to use as Samson did.
Find it. Use it, with great discretion
And only in love – not in hate.
4:14 a.m.
Meditation is not magic
nor is it key to creation's treasures
but merely small step in direction
of self control of distractions
many which do abound.
Nay – such power be not for fools,
to squander at any whim
but there for true believers,
pure of heart and purpose
other than self aggrandizement.
Listen to the children,
for they have much to say,
of love and of reality.
4:18 a.m.

George Eliot

July 14, 1996 @ 2:45 a.m.

Earth – home place of humanity –
perfect in every way for persons to live,
is also home to multitude of living creatures –
animals and not.
To despoil its beauty and function is most regrettable.
No other planet has its unique qualities.
Its undoing will be humanity's greatest loss.
Once unbalanced, such gyrations of weather
and crustal involvement will be
unprecedented in human history records.
Life and living is an opportunity most special and unique.
2:52 a.m.
My home is very different and very far in time.
Our journey was made possible by translocation,
a concept and theory not yet known to science.
Only few among humanoids
are able to manage this technology.
Fortunately for other beings,
that organized groups with adequate resources
have not yet acquired or mastered this process,
for such destructive qualities has
quarantined your planet and species to all except
monitors such as myself and party.
2:58 a.m.
Someday you will understand this process.

As all processes, it is ambivalent to its use.
Surely your organized governments
would use this technology to destroy other states
and their own in so doing. Time is on our side.
Such technology is unobserved and unutilized.
Those who master this process will be exterminated,
of necessity, by our patrols.
We cannot allow a species such as yours to destroy our galaxy.
3:03 a.m.

Alien being

Transcriber's note:
Translocation is a mass displacement technique in which random molecular motion is biased and synchronized allowing for extremely rapid changes in direction and velocity with no negative effects on equipment or personnel. The other component of translocation is the miniaturization of space expansion of electron orbits in one direction, by taking advantage of the ability of an object or atom to be in two places at the same statistical instant.

July 16, 1996 @ 5:09 a.m.

Time, measure of all thought,
cadence of life and death,
exists as king, ruler of logic,
but are not logical by nature but intuits.

Slaves to temporary temporal bodies,
most un–perfect and un–enduring.
These enslave us and confine our true nature.
Glimpse true self and begin freedom's march slowly –
slowly – one confinement at a time –
heaped upon each other.
This be life's greatest challenge – yet undertake it.
5:14 a.m.
Lust is body's language of procreation.
Unbridled, it knows no bounds,
is totally without logic and as such is key
to understanding your true nature.
Channel lust and you can enslave enslavement.
Enlightenment is not liberation from lust
but a direct result of re–directing that powerful longing
for liberation from time's grip.
In lust – time is subdued and our true nature is revealed.
5:19 a.m.
Other driving forces are mere shadows of lust,
and less powerful and more elusive.
Fear not lust – cut it loose to liberate
and free you from dominion of mind and time.
Be not victim and enslaved to its measure and to its beat.
Seek freedom from within and all things will be revealed
through pursuit of freedom from enslavement
to time itself.
5:23 a.m.

Francis Bacon

July 17, 1996 @ 5:38 a.m.

This cry be heard from such far place
that none there be that liveth couldst
be done, now, then or anytime.
With what few breath be I allowed
to speak, afore parted be again for evermore.
Hear these words and take to heart
such recommendations as doth quick thee heart.
Transgressions be at thine own expense.
Never at another's.
Thy brother art thy self and no other.
Treat each and every other as thy self –
for tis sadly true. That which doest thou to tother –
doest thou in reality to thyself for eternity.
Strange but simple truth this be.
If no other take thee from this effort,
be thou far the richer for it.
Curse not for in so doing –
cursed thee become at thine own expense
and waste of time it be most profound.
5:43 a.m.
Time ticks not for those now dead
and in hand of own where punishment
for such oversight be most enduring and unpleasant,
with special 'tention paid to thy dislikes
which happen repeatedly with no delights.

Tread not lightly on another,
for tread thee upon thyself most forcefully forever
in barren land and place most unpleasant.
Hinder not another for in so doing harkin hindering
of such great desertion that hinder not again
will thoust ever but only be hindered.
Time be thy enemy for ticketh not to thy liberation
from such disgust as cannot be imagined.
Take advantage of thy opportunity.
Cast seeds of love along thy path
to bloom with thy passing in death eternal.
5:52 a.m.

Sir John William Scott

5:52 a.m.
I am better now, more composed
and able to move about.
No longer do I suffer pain
and anguish, dissolution and desire.
Here shall I reside in thy secret garden
till complete and whole again,
if ever that tis to pass.
Such pleasant place, peaceful
and filled with thy handiwork.
Tis most civil and appreciated much
what thou hast done for me –
stranger no longer, but best of friend –

as best as any couldst wish for.
Here will I shower thee and thine
with love and peace.
Be'est thou now content,
for from this place will emanate
such strength as none canst imagine.
Birds 'n' bee alike twill bless this place
with their visit.
Thy request – if possible to bestow,
twill be my pleasure to grant and assist thee.
See my face. Sense my beauty,
lost and now retrieved – by friendship
most sincere as friend and servant.
5:57 a.m.

Robin, thy truest friend

July 18, 1996 @ 2:59 a.m.

Walk freely about dressed in flowing white.
Take in all there is to take.
Step lightly upon the grass so green.
Praise the living earth for such liberty,
for such may not always be.
String thyself into eternity.

Fear not for thou art safe here
among the murdock and columbine.
Gather 'tention from all time –
for unique among all beings art thou – Robin
for none to my knowledge hath ever
this feat accomplished – nor even tried.
Most interesting and unique.
None seems to mind ensnarement and dissemination
of thoughts past or present
merely opportunity in passing –
strung like spider web through time, space and reality.
Most intriguing and delightful.
3:06 a.m.
3:07 a.m.
Such wanderings a man maketh
in search of justice and peace of mind
is truly beyond imagining –
even for one so traveled
and well wandered a soul such as mine.
Time is not an issue,
but twould be most helpful and beneficial
to know when such wandering is to end.
I suppose what replaces endless wandering
is better known than appreciated,
but pleasant oasis art thou,
shimmering, translucent and inviting

across the sands of time – more than a mirage.
Thou art illusion not, but certainly illusory,
glinting with thy beauty most inviting and translucent.
Fair thee well Robin.
3:15 a.m.

John S. Wasserman

July 19, 1996 @ 2:30 a.m.

Reversal of all things is the rule.
Nothing is done that is not undone.
No injury goes uninjured in return –
Always this is the case without exception.
To condone injury to another condones injury to self.
This simple lesson is often overlooked
or forgotten in zealous zeal for injury real or imagined.
Any priest or religious leader
who seeks violence against another
on religious grounds
is a false prophet with devil's tongue,
2:36 a.m.
and shall suffer such humiliation
and despair in the depths of Hell
as one cannot begin to imagine.

Each action begets reaction
which is far greater in consequence –
till all are blind and deaf and dead.
Must you never learn this simple truth.
Each man is window to soul of God.
Injury to any is insult to all.
Such evil and such violence begets
more evil and more violence –
none escapes from justice – never.
2:41 a.m.

Horace B. Anderson III

July 20, 1996 @ 5:17 a.m.

Mothers cry out in anguish for their lost children.
Their curse shall follow those into Hell and beyond.
Such vengeance knows no rest.
Every second shall cry out for torture
and penetration of their shell.
Safety is unknown from their wrath.
Forgiveness – never.
Those and their offspring shall know no peace,
even in death, when devils take them
to their just reward in Hade's depths

whence anvils ring in constant inner pain.
5:22 a.m.
Of such is conflict born and thus continues.
Mothers' mercy be only cure –
but none will be forthcoming –
and so the violence continues,
until every eye be gouged
and every tongue ripped out.
Pity is such waste of time and talent.
Some great evil lurks with finite purpose
to rend all mankind
and purge planet of such desecration.
To what end – what purpose has man come?
5:26 a.m.

Hugh O'Brien Esq.

July 24, 1996 @ 5:09 a.m.

Toddlers, twinklers and travelers –
all share a common zeal
for similar encounters
with new and enchanting things –
tall and thin, with elfin ears –
a permanent smile

and muffler in summer.
Each gremlin and ghoul can likewise
be of interest to them all –
indiscriminate , faithful to their fate,
with not a care to be had,
these toddlers travelers and tikes.
5:14 a.m.

Joyce Simpson Riley, Mother Goose

July 28, 1996 @ 8:39 a.m.

Jonas Caribe – Born in 1793 – Portuguese –
Went by ship to Africa – Not a sailor –
Kilt 29 men – some black some not –
Traded women and children –
Got sick with fever –
in his third year in Africa – Ivory Coast –
Did not know he was / is dead
and suffering in purgatory –
Full beard, bushy hair –
reddish tint to brown thick hair –
Angry man – Long since dead.
8:46 a.m.

August 9, 1996 @ 5:01 a.m.

Shoes – shoes of the fisherman.
These are all that direct my way.
From time immemorial,
those shoes have danced for me
to tap out life's direction, cadence and song.
Even now those shoes sing to me,
tell me what to do and what to not do.
They have never let me down.
Even as a child those shoes guided me
through many tracks and mistakes,
but always, they were there for me.
Those shoes may not be adequate for your journey,
but for me, they made possible the trip.
No religious man was I, but guided –
always guided by those shoes –
clop, clop, clop.
4:20 a.m.

A. Quinn

August 13, 1996 @ 5:01 a.m.

Torment, pain and suffering –
this I knew first hand.
Such anguish all around. Nothing grew.
From within this darkened room,
small tentacles sprouted
and became my roots – my life – my hope.
These roots bound me to the tree of life
which became central to my life.
Now, that all pain is gone,
I can honestly say life was good to me.
Life gave me the chance which others were denied.
My affliction was my strength.
My anguish was the kernel
which became love for all
and joy for none.
To you I now pass this secret.
5:08 a.m.
Give nothing of thyself,
or dead will you be in short order
from drainage of life's succor.
Allow God's energy and information to freely pass
without resorting to comment or to judgment.
Root your sense of self in pure and honest purpose
to be God's messenger,

to give each what power, what information, what love,
what health or whatever is passed through you
to them from beyond the pale.
Force nothing.
Give freely when asked.
Give nothing unasked for.
These are my secrets for eternal life and eternal health.
5:14 a.m.

Vana

August 14, 1996 @ 5:07 a.m.

Crime and punishment, cannot now be mitigated by home rule but requires an approach wholly new, not withstanding old tried and true but failed methods. Crime comes from within the individual and is not created by society at large. The opportunity for crime or not crime is created by society. To move to the position that less and less is crime and less and less is punishment is erroneous in principle, but attractive to liberal and lunatic alike. To move to position of total free will, with no societal consequence for action taken, seems lunacy at its core but in fact is the method, which insures the ultimate success sought by all. Society defines crime. To itemize and itemize crimes increases both opportunity and code of ignorance for crimes to occur. To abolish penal codes in favor of individual ethics and behavior with total personal responsibility will assure future safety and security for all.

5:17 a.m.

In transition, judges should be given total freedom to interpret what is acceptable and what is unacceptable – and crime should not pay and should not be profitable, for there in lies total motivation. Punishment should be flexible and punishment should be quick and appropriate. To kill is to be killed. To rape is to be raped. To beat is to be beaten. To rob is to be robbed. To cheat is to be cheated. To vandalize is to be vandalized. To harm others is to be harmed in return. Life liberty and the pursuit of happiness is precious and mob rule by ignorance cannot be allowed.

5:23 a.m.

George Patton

August 15, 1996 @ 4:53 a.m.

4/3 A B = distance between realities

Where: B = time traveled

And A = BBB… to the nth

Where N = the square of velocity in nanoseconds

Thus 4/3 (BBB…B) B = Destination

4:56 a.m.

Einstein

August 19, 1996

Could no more be said.
His time had come.
Here are numbers of your destiny so inclined.
To others help as I now do you – 1–7–22–11–8–
Enjoy what is God given.
Help others. For tis written –
He who helps a small child helps mankind.
In so doing, he helps himself.
8:23 a.m.

Vangelia

August 26, 1996 @ 3:00 a.m.

Time to talk – to tell a tale–
that turns your blood to cold snail–
creeping slow through yer body
and yer soul–where entrail meets the past–
where present and future be same– be same–
fur once I was like you
afore I died and now reside
in heavens hall
which– be different– very different

than you been told
where dead men's souls
and dead man's mind often collide.
3:04 a.m.
6:41 a.m.
To my left– to my right–to my all around –
Imaginary imaginings of every kind.
That's what frightens.
That's what make you kneel.
Please God spare me from my imaginings.
Spare me from them so real – so real.
Before me, behind me – on top as well.
These are now my world.
Hope is hope but hope won't help –
not today – for tomorrow never comes
and yesterday never was.
Hope is good but just won't do
when all your imaginings are real,
are real, and after you.
A gun, a gun,
that's what I need,
but bang, bang, bang –
the bullets are imagined
and nothing happens to my imaginings
but they do get mad – very mad
when a gun is pointed at them –

Wouldn't you?
A knife, a sword or giant stick –
These really make them mad.
That's when your imaginings come for you –
6:50 a.m.
Since hope is gone – and guns won't do –
Since sticks and stones and knives won't too.
I'm doomed– I'm doomed.
I guess I must give up –
and make friends with all my imaginings –
Wouldn't you?
6:52 a.m.

Theodore Seuss Geizel

Being dead isn't so bad – but these imaginings.
What's a folk to do ??

August 27, 1996 @ 4:55 a.m.

I wish to speak.
My name is Sam – Samuel Livingstone.
I really shouldn't be here, you know.
I really shouldn't.
Tell them I'm sorry. I'm really sorry.
This was just a big mistake.
I really shouldn't be here.

I should be alive like everybody else,
but no, this had to happen.
This was an accident you know.
Now look at me. What a mess.
My whole life is a complete mess.
Just because of that silly game.
It was an accident you know.
This was an accident.
5:00 a.m.
It is very dark here.
I hate the dark.
Nothing – no wind – no rain – no smell – nothing.
I'm stuck here in the dark.
I have something that I'm hanging onto.
It's like a wall made out of thick rope
with holes between the ropes.
The walls are like a big netting,
a giant netting.
Something washes over me every so often.
Sooner or later it will break my grip
and I will be washed away, to who knows where.
I should be still alive.
I didn't mean for this to happen.
5:04 a.m.
Don't leave me.
I have been here ever since I woke up.
I remember the loud pop – the whack –
the thud of hitting the pavement and the swoosh.

This powerful wind rushed past me in a great wave
and I was sucked into this vortex –
this tunnel of darkness.
Sooner or later my grip will fail.
Then I'll be a goner.
I should have just stayed at home
and drank my beer and watched the game.
Damn!
Why did I have to sneak out like that for a snort –
just one snort.
What a bitch.
5:09 a.m.

August 29, 1996 @ 5:17 a.m.

Yes, I would like to make a statement. I hope that my contribution was significant and lasting. To see into the future is not possible for mortal man. To establish lasting tradition of substance and duration – founded in solid American history is all one hopes for. I do not know what has transpired in my absence. Some of what I have done may still preside. Much of what I tried to do has certainly changed. My admonition is that each American be proud and strong.

5:22 a.m.

That each American have opportunity – solid education in classics and in theory. That each American be rooted in religion and love of God – love of country and love of fellow man. These are the foundations of true and lasting democracy.

5:25 a.m.

God's speed, Theodore Roosevelt

August 30, 1996 @ 2:07 a.m.

"Hell – the best thing I ever did was drop that 'A' bomb on those Japs. They would still be dug in somewhere shooting our boys. You know this is good damn farmland. You can grow anything in Kansas. All you need is a little rain – Yes sir – just a little rain. All a man needs is a chance to work.

2:11 a.m.

If ya don't wanna work – then ta hell with ya. Government otta get out yer way and let ya rip. You know this is damn good soil. This here Kansas dirt – best damn farming country 'n the world. Piss on them politicians. Not a one of em worth a damn."

2:14 a.m.

Harry Truman

August 31, 1996 @ 1:35 a.m.

Gilmour – John Patrick Gilmour – That be my name.
To thank you is what I should do – for floundering was I.
Thrashing about in that darkness and water.
I was a goner for sure and certain.
Where did this island come from?
I thought sure I was in the middle of an ocean.
1:39 a.m.
The sand is nice – and dry.
I thought is was very windy and rainin'.
Strange – very strange – I saw no light.
Here there be fire – quite warm and bright.
This is strange – unexpectedly strange
but thanks once again for the helpin' hand.
The sea can be a terrible place
to the uninformed
and overboard –
without ship or provisions.
1:43 a.m.
Can I be of service to ya?
Gratitude is all I have at the moment
but of that I'll freely give all you can ask fer.
You don't talk much.
Yer clothes are funny and spare

but any helpin' hand in the midst of a storm
is a helpin' hand and welcome at that.
My Mary sent me off to sea in search of prosperity –
almost drowned did I
but fortunately you saved me skin fer another day.
1:47 a.m.
Mary certainly appreciates your help and assistance.
Strange – my clothes be dry already –
and warm through and through am I.
That isn't the hint of morning sun on the horizon is it?
This has been quite the finding.
I don't hear the sloshing of the sea any longer.
Just the quiet of day before first light.
If ya spoke a little I would be more at ease
but never question the man who just saved yer life.
Sit awhile afore the cock crows.
1:52 a.m.
My memory fails me.
How ever did I end up here in the first place?
1:53 a.m.

YOU DIED MY FRIEND. YOU DIED!

September 4, 1996 @ 5:44 a.m.

As I look down upon the grave injustice wrought upon the people – by government awry. My heart is burdened that any such great nation as ours – could be led so far astray of justice, peace and tranquility by the godless minority. Sick at heart and heavy rancor – with great disgust I view from on high – the grave consequences that lie before such nation

5:48 a.m.

that allows such power and decision to slip into hands so weak and self serving. None should ever wear the banner of president of this great nation who in weakness and lack of fortitude brings the whole nation to the brink of disaster with malice and missing character. God has given each and every one the gift of reason. Do not abandon that gift – and do not abandon this nation in search of personal gain.

5:54 a.m.

Too many have died in effort to honor, justice and freedom. How can any just man sleep when such injustice is heaped upon nations and citizens alike by – the powerful upon the meek. Rise up fellow citizens. Take back the helm of this great nation from those who would wreck this great ship of state, upon the watery graves of millions at the very gates of Hell.

5:59 a.m.

Abe Lincoln

September 6, 1996 @ 1:30 a.m.

Tis shame great as any be –
that with horses such as these–
and carriage – most handsome –
that none there be
which art smart enough
to know which end to 'arness
and which she blows.
A shame as great as any –
that men there be
who wouldst cut men down
for nothing other – with bayonet or spear –
or shot of grape – or musket ball.
Tis shame as great as any
which could befall –
any of the king's men.
Tis such a shame –
tragedy as great as any
which could befall man or beast.
Tis shame as great as any –
which could befall the poor soul
who be sent to Amerikee –
to be cut down before his time
by whores and sluts and rotten wine
and vermin for men

who shoot from neath bridge
or behind barn.
1:38 a.m.
or narrow ditch with pellet o' lead –
as deadly as any which could be shot
from any king's men –
with shattered gun of solitude.
A pity as great as any
which could befall any man
to be cut down
and never mourned in Amerikee.
A pity as great as any
which could befall any man.
1:41 a.m.

Journeyman

September 12, 1996 @ 5:11 a.m.

I am he who hath been called from afar
to sing in silence but to spout forth rhyme
n reason as none before nor since.
My name is William Shakespeare.
He who writ verse most perfect and prolific –

but accompanied always by this lovely voice from within.
This tale has not been told nor retold
by mouths of men nor tongues any.
Tis old as old. Tis new as new.
But never afore mentioned by me
nor any other in passing.
So be it.
Now from beyond time speaks William Shakespeare.
Now long since dead and none the better for it.
5:17 a.m.,

SERPENTINE

Rogue of rogue, thieve of thieves,
who with smile sublime
rode he never upon back of ass
nor whore of bine
Serpentine medallion upon his breast
blacken velvet his true colour
never white nor any other
with beard most full and bushy
hat down low upon his eye
never smiling yet beguiling
rode he forth upon equine stallion
of chestnut colour most striking and handsome
never speaking but with his sword
he kilt men – many men – and women too
with serpentine sword or snake with his choosing
most feared and hated – most admired
the rider black who slew all before him in unlike fashion
5:24 a.m.
men were cut to bone with swift and deadly sword
not so lucky – women –
whose souls were cut and carried off
to live and die with none such guidance
nor remorse any for sinful ways
the life of lepers cut off from all that liveth

by pain of parting from one such Serpentine
5:28 a.m.
Till death in squalor – upon them visit till his dying day
Such life he lived he lived most consistent
yet none mourned with his passing
as now none my condition – here in Hades corner small
upon the cask where fell he in dying death
was marked in blackest ink
Serpent bold with gleaming eye and tongue most forked
That none should touch nor ever tread
the blacken casket of Serpentine
5:33 a.m.
With gaff and grapple – did he fall
to meet his maker by death's call
Serpentine in cask of casket so entwined
Was slew by cabin boy most virtuous
which he touched with sword not
but snake saved only for women
So was his destiny to be his undoing
Invincible with sword or screw
Until attempted to undue
boy of innocence with serpentine screw
tripping in his arrogance
upon the net of debauchery
spread long ago for unsuspecting souls
to end their reign of terror in pain and anguish.

5:39 a.m.
Buried deep in sea so cruel
with jack 'n grapple for weight and dine
so met his maker Serpentine.
Beneath the keel of all good ships
remains of mark of Serpentine.
Cold steel or hot screw
could save not the likes of Serpentine
doomed in his excellence
to misuse gifts of perfection
and thus be undone
The undoing of Serpentine
greatest sword and greatest screw.
5:43 a.m.

William Shakespeare

September 19, 1996 @ 3:25 a.m.

Truly great men live by the rule of law.
Not man's law but God's law, natural law.
The law of giving, the law of love and respect
for all things great or small.
3:28 a.m.

Mark Twain

3:40 a.m.
What happens to men who murder
and do other violent things
and what happens to their victims?
Murderers beware –
for time stops with each click o' clock.
Murder never pays –
for such heavy price must be paid in like kind
that boggles any mind.
3:43 a.m.
Victims remain a site of infliction
till all endurance be lost to time and remembrance.
Till that passes – yet they die again daily
and each minute – till time ceases.
Such pain and affliction – be born and reborn
until culprit has no pain left un–endured –
tis such great sadness and grief that none can imagine.
3:47 a.m.

Robin, thy twin in heart

3:58 a.m.
Behind every window there is a glass.
Behind every mirror there is a door.
The glass is a window to past, present and future.
The mirror is a door to each and every place and time.
The secret is in the handle.

The secret is in the door.
The secret is in the turning –
just so much and no more.
4:03 a.m.

Tyreillius 705 BC

September 21, 1996 @ 12:29 a.m.

Harold Hawright

Most of the time I just drink and carry on.
But last night I got a little out of hand.
It was an accident – nothing planned.
They were Mexicans – so it ain't so bad –
but it was an accident.
Damn they were pretty.
I thought they liked me.
I didn't mean to hurt no body.
Don't be telling on me now Tommy.
It was just an accident.
12:34 a.m.
Hell man – I didn't mean to hurt no body.
I don't know what happened.
Give me another one.

I need some extra tonight.
Get me another whole pitcher.
Drown your sorrow that's what I say.
12:36 a.m.

Austin, Texas

September 30, 1996 @ 3:30 a.m.

Conditions are ripe for rebellion.
Snow is deep in the passes.
Enemy troops are within striking distance
from our heartland.
Swiss army units are at the ready –
Poised but hopeful that this battle will not come to pass.
Only God knows what the morrow shall bring.

Love as always. Yours dearly,
Samuel King, Left. Col. 3rd Brigade

October 2, 1996 @ 5:15 a.m.

Nigh on to 20 years ago,
I came t'here with nothing.
Look at t'her now.
This tis mighty fine 'n–deed.
Such a beauty.
All this is mine.
Folks 'n back holm twould not b'lieve –
such as me could hav'n such a fine place.
Not ev'n a fence – nor rock –
as far as the eye can see.
Now tis time to fetch me a woman.
A real woman from home.
Not one of these floozies from the way station nor bar.
A real woman with proper upbringing
and pretty white skin from back home.
5:23 a.m.

John Foster Mc Dermitt

October 4, 1996 @ 5:32 a.m.

Dem dat twas dat et der pi–
Whads wrse fur beer ter eyds –

Tis talid sord derf tis olf ot surf rum di–
wit bur sur nied clemst widh fur pur n out.
Clems dem der wats enflieg wits fun.
5:36 a.m.
Slk un fir dour – sig un crafs –dis n crafs zieg –
nine – ere wats endur –
per ol wid nur en sorid heil –
und otts dos liven zig en unden seilf –
widt zen dur floggen –werst zen truf –
ben zer win nine sur floggen –
nine de floggen – enz – sulden kortz –
nine der floggen kortz – et surf –
elden zaf – wid – non pulzen kommphzen –
en zulden tyne.
En mine de umlaggen – mine de zoloff.
5:44 a.m.

October 5, 1996 @ 2:04 a.m.

Und sig – braken en un reofkin –
churchen kinder brachen zen ter –
durleof – ze stackhousen –
mit nine zoelof nor brenchin –
chenrquen zut worlefinten nine

ze mortif zeigen e nine progerton –
wit stolifen mit non vermenzorgen.
2:16 a.m.
I have no idea what this is or is not or says or says not.

October 8, 1996 @ 1:41 a.m.

I can feel things – not just imaginings –
not just with the aid of your fingers.
I can actually feel physical objects.
I am becoming reality.
It is working.
I am becoming real, not imagined or imaginings,
Not just conjured nor conjuring's.
What an adventure.
1:44 a.m.

Robin

October 10, 1996 @2:11 a.m.

From utter chaos comes deceit – most profound –
prolific frustration from the triangle of doom

glistens with porous hope
with oblivion as thy partner in sleep.
Count not on extrication where none doth reside.
Come quietly in night on bended knee
to view thyself as at the brink –
with deep water – cool and black
to lure thee on to disaster.
From this water springs forth fountain of eternal life –
with death its silent partner
in ether foul and stench so retched.
Smile once more before the chill of death
freeze thy contorted face for time eternal.
2:17 a.m.
I am black as death.
This portal through which shines eternal life
as pearl most precious and benign.
Look deep into the waters of defeat and debauchery –
for not a single cloud of white shall be thy rescue –
only emptiness forever from the void of time.
All is not lost.
All is not wasted –
but futility abounds in realm of time.
Take thy brief respite from eternity as gift or curse –
for none the difference does it make.
Mine eyes look backward down the trail of time –
to see all left undone and done as well.

Count not thy hours as blessings
but as opportunities lost to eternity.
Come my friend – in death and desperation.
2:24 a.m.

Edgar Allen Poe

October 11, 1996 @ 6:31 a.m.

I would that your heart were torn in two
than two by two by two by two
To be pierced by fright in night
Than by poisoned arrow in flight
None other hath such sorrow given
as thine own tongue 'gainst thy teeth
Twere not magic – but mere deceit
far worse than any crime – tis passion

B. J. Browne

October 12, 1996 @ 5:58 a.m.

Darkening skies forebode disaster

but none is extant
only time – the restless wanderer
chipping at these walls
chink – chink chink – chink,
till all is level again
Birds drop their duty
upon the face of man
who defileth all things
Such we call order
chaos to all living things
save man the tinkerer
6:02 a.m.

Evert Young Smith, Blacksmith and idolater

October 14, 1996 @ 1:02 a.m.

I say – now this is nice.
And who might you be?
Come hither Agatha.
Here – look at this –
small creature that thou art.
Who are you ?
From whence came you ?
Why disturb us at table ?

Can't you see –
we are dining on this fine fowl –
legs akimbo –
with fine fruit and such good wines.
How did you get here ?
You are interesting aren't you ?
Yes – yes – not real are you –
ghostly and translucent
as though from some other place 'n time –
dumb – very dumb.
Can't you talk ?
Windows from another place and time.
1:08 a.m.
See Agatha –
this creature –stares unblinking at us –
stealing our very thoughts –
extracting our very words.
Probably sweeping them to some other place 'n purpose.
God knows what.
Agatha, can't you see the little vermin –
all silvery and translucent with unblinking eyes ?
I have nothing of the kind –
barely touched the wine.
You must be blind Agatha dear –
for I swear there is a ghostly creature of some kind
staring out upon me from neath this chair.

OK ! I shant have another drop.
Very fine wine though –
very fine indeed.
1:13 a.m.
You know Agatha – he or it –
Probably reports directly to God –
or some devil or perhaps –
another time 'n place.
Yes that's it –
A spy from some other time –
sent to spy out our secret lives –
of indulgence and debauchery.
Isn't that an interesting thought –
that some would care so much as to spy us out
and seek kinky secrets from our lair ?
1:17 a.m.
I find this most intriguing.
How could that be done ?
To sneak across time –
to steal into our private quarter –
to ferret out juicy morsel
as would turn the king's blood to boil
and have us all excommunicated from his sacred church
or burn us at stake –
for some unimagined foul deed of wicked proportion.
This thief of time and place

could spy perhaps for our beloved king–
ass among men that he be.
Be gone.
Be gone –spy of spies –
Lest my sanity forsakes me.
1:22 a.m.

Henry Wadsworth Longfellow

October 16, 1996 @ 4:00 a.m.

Ezra Keats on his death bed

My time has been spent in effort
to catalog human experience and emotion.
Far better to have spent it wisely
on living and laughter.
Too soon life's engine – stops
in throes and purr.
Too soon the casket lid –
closes eyes from seeing such magic that is life.
All in all it was a good life –
But rather wasted on intellectual pursuit
When for but a dime and a little time –
I could have been a Bill Brown or Tom Snee.

For but a smile and a little guile –
I could have been a lover too.
4:05 a.m.
Tis sad – but true –
but now is not the time to change
–the little things I do –
for now is my time to die
and I should concentrate upon the task at hand.
By the way – who are you ?
In dapper hat and spotted shoe.
The likes of you I've not seen before nor never again.
Are you death – come to dance at my expense ?
Fever has so weakened this old hulk of once a man.
Take some time to enjoy life.
Give yourself the day off –
and kill another, not me.
4:11 a.m.

Ezra Jack Keats

October 21, 1996 @ 1:15 a.m.

Here's the way it is. Every time a change or an action takes place – it also doesn't take place. The time thread that memory is attached to is what makes up your reality – your dimension. But the field of total possibility still exists and has not changed by that decision or by that action. To understand this fact and this phenomena – is to grasp the straws of creation. To give oneself freedom to choose or not choose – to give oneself the option of re–choosing or as it were, re–shuffling the deck, not only makes all possibilities possible but makes any possibility possible or even re–possible. You can change an event before it happens or even after it happens, because the total field of all possibility has not been changed

1:22 a.m.

– only your insistence on a single time line has changed and this and this alone binds your reality to any particular course of action or particular outcome. To understand this simple concept is to understand the nature of reality. To give yourself freedom to choose or not choose or to even un– choose – gives you total freedom that is your birthright as a spiritual being of unlimited potential. Bind not your future to such a scheme as would your fellow travelers insist upon. Free yourself. Choose in luxury, and total

1:28 a.m.

oblivion to any time line – however imposed – by self or other. There in lies the heart of magic and disbelief. There in lies your distinction as greatest seer and greatest healer that thou art. Even I, long since dead and buried am now resurrected totally changed in your presence. Total responsibility means total freedom. Lack there of means total enslavement and utter chaos. Choose to see me as I am. See me as the radiant creature of beauty and of light which you have liberated and transformed by your diligence and creativity. See me – for I am Robin thy truest friend and confidant, most splendid and most beautiful.

1:35 a.m.

Robin

October 24, 1996 @ 2:59 a.m.

I was not by name so given, Hunchback of Notre Dame.
Nor was I in fact a real hunchback.
Nor did I inhabit the belfry of Notre Dame.
I was in fact, in service at Notre Dame as servant,
and did serve as stimulus
for the creation of the character Quasimodo,
though that was not my name.
in fact I was loyal and faithful servant
to church and council alike all the days of my life –
and in fact died in accident later in life.
My one great love was Notre Dame itself,
and to that divinely inspired structure
devoted my entire life.
She was and remains my one great love.
3:07 a.m.

John

October 25, 1996 @ 1:41 a.m.

Godless creature of the night.
Wench with tongue of brazen fire.
Why hast thou descended upon me pitiless.
Canst thou see I bear no arms

nor burden any man least thee.
Surely thou hast mistaken me
for another of lesser birth and more gall.
My time here be most limited.
Vex me not vixen with devil's tongue.
Be gone afore I thrash thee with casing of urchin
or slam thy face with klaxon fist
or muzzle thee with cheap wine
or worse yet.
Send king's men upon thee
to make thee whore which thou art.
Bitch among men of honor
and colour of Queen's knights.
Get thee hence.
1:47 a.m.
Such splendid bitch thou art.
Bed thee would I with great pleasure
were thy tongue silent or ripped out.
How God could belch up such combination
of beauty and bitch
bends mind to task for ever brought.
Wife thou art truly bane to man and beast alike.
I would love thee more if thy tongue would give me rest
and my purse would'st thou not sever from my vine.
1:52 a.m.

Byron, Lord

October 28, 1996 @ 2:27 a.m.

I feel more solid.
I feel more complete.
My faculties are returning to me.
Once more I can think.
What an adventure that was.
I'm still lacking in some essence,
but all in all I'm much better now.
Objects have dimension and colour –depth and texture.
No longer mere shadows of surrealism.
2:30 a.m.
Soon my mind will be at capacity and once again
can I take on complex comparatives and dissertations.
Thank you so much for your assistance
in this matter so grave.
My heart shall always be open for you,
fine fellow that thou art – most splendid person,
seer and now it would seem – most splendid rescuer.
Such a dreadful place was that –Isle of Purgatory.
Even the wickedest of men
surely don't deserve to endure there.
Most happy am I to be thus gone
from that place of constant torture –
though it would seem I am still somewhat lacking,
but this process so contrived by thee

is most adequate to the task.
2:38 a.m.
Never could I have imagined or envisioned that you,
or any other could so remove me from my living Hell –
though most mild indeed compared
to those in greater depth
where fiends and demons
be constant companion to the evil doer.
Most graciously yours, Robin
Who now becomes Robin most complete –
and forever in thy service as friend and confidant,
ah to breath again the air of this lovely place
spared from ravages of devil's helpers.
2:44 a.m.

Robin,
thy truest friend and companion

October 29, 1996 @ 4:39 a.m.

I am dead and buried.
I wish to speak to you.
You who wish for the power,
the power to admonish the pains of evil.
Sinning is for sinners.

Neither here nor there.
The children will teach you.
Listen – listen to their song.
It is the song of life, of love, of happiness,
sung in sorrow for their dying world –
suffocated by the sins of the evil doer and the ignorant.
Pine not for better days, for none will come better
nor more prosperous than today.
This is the key to all doing and to all undoing.
Today is the only day there is –
God's gift to you –
God's gift to all living things.
Defile not this day on behalf of some other,
4:46 a.m.
real or imagined, that was or might be.
Today is all there is.
Make progress today. Make friends today.
Make happy today – for every other is imagined.
Let not cruelty, injustice and ignorance
of others – older and dumber –
spoil the beauty and serenity which is today.
Smile and the world is your friend.
Death awaits your every breath.
Don't waste a single one
on envy or poverty or discontent.
Breathe freely and with contentment
like every living thing

and life and love and happiness are yours.
4:52 a.m.
Wish not for that which is already yours.
Worry not and your gifts will appear,
as great as any that have been bestowed by God
upon the living or the dead.
Be of good cheer, for what appear as problems
are merely road signs on the highway of life.
4:54 a.m.

Your Aunt Vanga

P.S. God loves you.

October 30, 1996 @ 1:41 a.m.

In life and death, monetary value is of no consequence.
Only principle is at stake.
My time on earth is now past,
but my time at internment has but begun,
for I forsook friend and family in quest of monetary gain.
Such a fool was I, for now I suffer so for no pay.
Such remorse eternal for lack of heart and conscience –
Sad – sad am I for now I daily pay without benefit or end.
1:45 a.m.
Follow my good advice and bank on friendship,

kindness and self respect.
Bank not coupons nor coin but on deeds of common good
and value these most highly,
for no amount of interest or profit
will stave the scrivener's shaft
from piercing thine own eye
with greed and intolerance.
The season of merry making
and giving of gifts approach again.
The answer lies not in giving of gifts
but in giving one's heart and soul
with dignity and delight.
1:49 a.m.
Look not to packages nor stores for satisfaction.
Look deep within your own soul and ask
what greater gift can be given
than to love and be loved,
for there lies the secret path to forgiveness
for omission and all other traits of excess.
Give not with hand nor purse but give of thy goodness,
Give self and give selflessly to each and all,
for they are truly brothers.
They are true reflections of thy self.
1:54 a.m.

J.P. Morgan

2:15 a.m.
Armageddon comes.
Seven years will pass before life resumes –
much changed in purpose and content.
No resources will be at thy disposal
during those seven years–no power –
no food – no communication.
Many must perish.
In their passing lies a future much different
for man and mankind.
Prepare, for even now the forces of greed and evil
push all towards the brink of disaster and collapse.
Time will cease for civilized man for seven years.
2:20 a.m.
Take this warning not as evidence but as advice.
Prepare, for the new age is dawning.
Know this and be saved – not from purgatory –
but from extinction which you so justly deserve.
2:22 a.m.

Jona

October 31, 1996 @ 3:01 a.m.

Insight is one thing, ability is another,
but skill is yet another thing entirely.
To be master of any, requires mastery of all.
Gifts are given. Gifts are used. Gifts are abused.
Striking the balance between all
requires great practice and greater perseverance.
Tis true – many gifts have been given
but the proper use requires much practice
and even greater forbearance.
To share or not is the heart of the issue.
To know is one matter.
To tell, quite a different issue.
3:07 a.m.
More than happy would I be to share
that which has been garnered
from years of practice and of patience –
yet if for one instant think that this will bring acceptance
or joy to you, then much surprise awaits.
No man can do these things without reproach.
Isolation is gift in return for such sharing.
None other but you – understands that these gifts
though much practiced and well intentioned –
shall not be so received.
3:12 a.m.

Expect nothing in return for your troubles –
for nothing shall be forthcoming –
but sense of satisfaction in gifts well used –
but not abused –
of sullen encounter with fellow men –
for none wishes to know the hour of his parting
nor even less the price for his past deed
in real and honest term. A blessing to thee I give
for none such shall come from family or friend–
less still from your fellow men.
3:17 a.m.

Michel de Nostredame (Nostradamus)

6:58 a.m.

Each time we meet –
I gain added strength and reality.
See my shoes. I have shoes –
pointed – beautiful and red.
Things are real to my touch –
no longer mere shadows of their former selves.
How long before I am truly and totally extricated
from that place of never ending purge –
I know not. But I dream not
nor do I have awareness of portions

remaining still in purgatory.
Yet quite certain am I that my totality is not yet here
where resides my friend of such immensity
and great skill that happy and contented am I
to so remain as long as you reside.
Smile for me.
Any problem that plagues thee can be but small
in comparison to what awaits the dead and dying –
and you are not of such.
This fine day is God given to you and all living creatures.
Enjoy that which is freely given in love.
7:06 a.m.

Your friend in time and eternity, Robin

November 1, 1996 @ 4:19 a.m.

Time immortal enemy can thou – I beseech thee –
spare me but a moment more –
afore I go to my just reward.
I care not that this mortal man I am –
give up the ghost or be incinerated – or fed to dogs.
Just spare me – just one moment more –
afore I go to be – longer with my dearest Abigail –
so lovely and so kind.

What with my passing shall become of her?
Time has spared her ravages
bestowed upon self and other
but nothing of myself shall remain –
cept miserable wretch that was I.
Dearest Abigail – forgive me one last time
for my transgressions
for time spares no one –
least me the wayward soul –
with gut shot wound of gun
to usher out my days in agony.
Surely hell can be no worse than taking leave of thee –
while with child – soon to bear
and not a single man to care
for thee and thine baby new born to be.
Share not my bed with any man
but save for me that place of honor
for I shall rest not till I return to thee
in nightly vigil eternal in death
Love eternal from – lover lost Abigail
4:31 a.m.

T. S. Eliot

November 3, 1996 @ 6:29 a.m.

Would that I could make such a statement.
Bear not arms nor anger against thy neighbor.
Bear not envy for purpose of control over any man.
Elevate thy women to place of honor.
Keep them safe for thy children's sake.
No law is so precious as to cost any man's life.
Kill or be killed is not reality.
Reality is – to injure is to be injured,
though that injury be slight or great.
Thy children matter most.
Give them knowledge.
Give them discipline.
Give them self respect.
Teach them the law of returns,
for all things returneth to the sender
with interest as thy penalty.
6:35 a.m.
Bear not false witness against thy neighbor or thy friend,
for in so doing plant seeds of thine own destruction.
Care not what any man believeth,
for all are adequate though none be accurate
in description of after–life.
Husband the earth and all its creatures,
for they are sacred.
To defile any creature is to defile thyself.

When death calls, be prepared
with open mind and clean hands.
Come not to the altar of God seeking parley,
for none such exists.
Bring the fortune of thy good deeds
as payment upon entry,
or demons will extract their due.
6:41 a.m.

Julius Caesar

November 4, 1996 @ 2:49 a.m.

Life and death are two different doors.
We come in one.
We breath awhile.
We go out the other.
What's the big deal?
The big deal is that, we still exist
on either side of both doors.
That indeed is a big deal.
If I had known this,
I would have taken more care while I was living,
Dying is O.K. but you keep right on going.
You just shuffle the deck and change the rules.
2:54 a.m.

A. B. Dick

November 4, 1996 @ 1:50 a.m.

When hours turn into days,
none shall escape these desperate days.
While cold steel and hot shot, blazes moon lit trench
the barren field calls, unworked from dawns light.
Tis evil most profane.
Unworked land cries out against a sullen statue
of men frozen dead in battle.
For what ?
What grave injustice hath thus reaped harvest
of young men younger than I?
What, is there no justice left 'pon the face of earth.
God surely sleeps while brother kills his brother
and rapes his brother's wife.
1:56 a.m.
Is there no shame?
Surely God demands that e'en I shall die,
untimely and in pain for such thought.
For I too have raped and plundered and burned,
with cannon and with grape.
Surely , devils will rise up from ash of my brother's land
and slew the lot of us that still cling tenaciously to life,
bloody toil that it is.
1:59 a.m.
My name matters not, for my deeds live on in infamy,

long after this corpse inhabit ditch or shallow grave,
scooped with empty hand from ravished land,
once called home.
Lincoln – give us peace, not war.
I can not further bear to so continue
as my brother's friend
and target for pistol 'n shot.
2:03 a.m.

P. J. Percy

November 6, 1996 @ 2:16 a.m.

These messages from beyond time cannot all be ignored,
for some will cut deep into your psyche,
to let out demons from childhood or religion,
or goad thee on to action.
No man can see these messages and be unmoved.
Time is not, time is naught.
Time is the ticker of your imagination,
the tocker of your dreams,
but none are real –
only imaginings, nothing more.
Pop out of the grove.
Look around.

Know that space and time are traps for your spirit
which is total and is free.
2:22 a.m.
Idiot that thou art,
choosing blindness over seeing –
deafness over hearing,
stupidity over enlightenment.
Awake before the cock crows its final cock.
Waste not another moment on invisible dreams
which matter not
for they are frivolous and without substance.
All that is – isn't,
Mere vibrations, nothing more –
mere imaginings – nothing more.
Must all be blind till not a one see
beyond that which tricks the mind into cadence.
The tune you hear is but the devil's lyre.
Awake before your hour of destruction.
2:27 a.m.

Allen B. Shumway

November 7, 1996 @ 12:14 a.m.

Who calls from beyond the portal?
Call me not from the damned,
lest thee too wish torture and replete.
What demon is you with pale face
and glazed watery eye?
Almost, but not quite alive, but neither dead.
Know ye not that I have great power here,
to rip out your eye and tear your throat –
brand thee forever with fire brand,
or burning coal that eats no flesh
but burns the soul forever.
Dare come to my domain,
thou squirrely ghost of wanna be.
Who art thou?
Can you not see my toil is real
with lost indigents and purple dead.
12:19 a.m.
I am king and commander of this realm
Depart spirit wanderer,
lest I burn out that tepid eye
with torch of eternal fire.
Bless nothing with your passing.
Touch nothing with your glass eye.
Get thee hence,

and respect for living and for dead –
neither of which art thou.
12:23 a.m.

Joel Demon and devil's helper

November 8, 1996 @ 4:00 a.m.

Out of darkness this thin ribbon of highway
guiding us from eternal damnation,
appears this tiny ribbon of hope,
a pencil of light in eternal darkness.
My voice precedes me into the light.
To follow this ribbon is my desire.
To extricate myself from eternal damnation,
but something holds me back.
I cannot make good my escape.
What radiant light,
what sense of peace, harmony and good will
emanates from this tiny light.
Surely there is hope of extrication.
Surely I cannot be damned eternally
with no sense of hope.
This heavenly straw must surely lead to liberation.
4:06 a.m.

Eternal damned

4:08 a.m.

My assessment of your situation is such that indeed though quite capable to function by your own wit, you are in need of some assistance. Your mind is so cluttered and lacking focus. With pleasure will I, shall I, assist you in this worthy effort, until need be to call upon my services.

Yours most kindly and with sincere regret,
Peter Hurkos

November 9, 1996 @ 1:20 a.m.

For a moment there, I sensed delusion or more,
perhaps indecision.
For nothing be worse than injustice to the wanderer–
nothing. Have you no decency left?
This be the question.
Know this and don't forget, that time is on my side
for I and I alone hold the secret to life eternal.
Nothing can be made less complicated than this fact.
Depart from me, evil makers,
for my day shall shine through clear and discreet
with none for fodder.
1:25 a.m.

Little is left undone.
Nothing much that matters.
None the less, time is still at issue.
Mark cadence with broom and twine,
but hear this out.
Time will liberate all that lives
and all that lives shall not die,
For death is mere trap of imaginings
which lures the spirit to turmoil and to test.
Giant step back from the precipice.
Count no man as idiot save thyself.
In total admonition and abandonment,
for when death kisses your fat lips
and licks your greasy face,
you too shall be liberated as any other.
Laugh if you like but it is true.
1:31 a.m.

Liberace

1:50 a.m.
Time the silent stalker,
stealing each day,
snipping on its way,
at any passing person or caretaker.

Giver of life and taker of death,
tumultuous at best,
sneakily at least,
lurid viewer of all that is but isn't.
Seek not divine intervention
where none exists,
but lure thy inner self,
with flame of reward
to taste fruits of imagination,
for this and only this
can free the fettered soul,
so fettered by mindless slavery
to clocks that tick
and tear away at eternal toil
to eke out mere living or sustenance little.
1:55 a.m.
But none the difference does this
or any other action taken or not,
make the slightest difference,
for in the end nothing changes
except the watch,
with new soldiers replacing old,
and old retiring to rot
in wait of death and ulcerated feet,
but in the end time ceases its eternal vigil
and eternity takes up its mantle,

for nothing really changes ,
only murder chases murderer
and vice chases visor, queens.
1:59 a.m.

John Scott Fitzgerald

2:00 a.m.
I begin these lines with one simple request,
that those whom I love,
from this day forward known as loved ones,
shall never be without,
though having things is having none.
To bear such burden
can cause ulcer of stomach
or headache to brow.
None the less tis my undying wish to forever,
from this moment have my seed sprout
and grow in garden of plenty.
Any man would want the same, no less
but toil shall not press its hand upon my seed
for all that wealth can buy,
shall they have and endure as best they can.
2:05 a.m.

Most sincerely, and graciously, in death as in life,

Sir John Whipple

2:06 a.m.
Lest any other take his turn afore me,
in message passed to living from us that now be dead.
Let this lesson be heard and learnt,
that dead is dead, but life ain't living.
So do your best but worry none the less
for none the difference makes.
Take time for fun and sport,
for be there none of that here.
Nothing but taskmaster takin' ye to task
for missing the mark and duty not done.
Live life as yer see fit,
cause in yer death be there plenty pain
to go around and last a long, long time.
2:10 a.m.

John (Dead man's Eye) Pope

November 10, 1996 @ 4:01 a.m.

From time immemorial comes life's deepest secrets. Time the cursor which moves all things. Without time there is no measure, no beat, there is only eternity. So time becomes the canvas upon which all actions are painted. Time is actually like a curtain which hangs loosely and has folds and wrinkles and is subject to gyrations driven by emotions from the origin of all things – God.

The wrinkles, the folds and the gyrations make possible some very interesting possibilities – further to complicate matters – each dimension has its own time curtain.

4:09 a.m.

These curtains stretch into infinity and have no edges in any direction but curve back upon themselves. Each dimension has its own peculiar shape and motion. These different dimensions overlap, intertwine and yet do not touch but form a complex meshwork which resemble a great ball of bird netting crumpled up, upon itself. Each action taken – or not taken –becomes attached to a time curtain and so forms a time line – essentially a string. These time lines, or strings when viewed in either direction appear to wander off in different directions weaving and waving without connection or discipline – undirected. But that is not the case. To fuse these strings or time lines, into a crystalline lattice (4:15 a.m.) is to create real and observable objects and phenomenon. The more points of fusion, the more dense or more real becomes the creation. For example, our dimension has six or seven points of fusion or more correctly, correlations which makes our world and our reality fairly light and airy compared with a dimension which has many points of fusion, say all twenty–six in its crystalline lattice.

4:21 a.m.

These connections or points of fusion are not static but instead, they are dynamic and subject to change. Some changes may be random, others are more focused and have specific purpose, i.e. time, height, width and depth. But these too are fluid and can be manipulated, discontinued, substituted for and folded back upon itself. To make this information of any value, functional value that is – one must first learn how to manipulate these quantities and make proper substitutions in order for (4:28 a.m.) there to be useful and predictable change. By working with a single strand at a time, it is possible to understand how these manipulations can be accomplished and what the predictable outcome will be. These rules are the tools of the creator and their use, proper or improper, begets creation as real as any natural creation or natural existence. The proper use of these tools, presents unlimited opportunities for man the thinker, man the tinkerer, man the creationist.

4:33 a.m.

Until we meet in time and space, yours most sincerely,

God

November 11, 1996 @ 1:38 a.m.

My trip to Hades seems over.
I feel most complete.
Though time the keeper and the taker,
shall set date for that departure,
not I, nor any man.
For to dwell in Hades corner and make escape,
is surely most untimely
and gainst the rule of fair play.
In love and season of eternity –
fairness is not the question – nor issue –
but escape – always.

Most happy and contented am I
to roam your estate, both day and night.
Companion your dogs 'n fish 'n birds –
and dare say –
scare thy neighbor with my wit and shadow.
For though truly a ghost not,
most assuredly do thus appear in nightly vigil
as chained and mortified as any ghost,
though in truth, am most free to go and do as I please.
1:45 a.m.
To what extent I so choose to visit –
To what extent I so choose – stay –
remains greatest mystery
that any man know, or better guess.
You have been most incredible
in my extraction from purge most severe.
For none there are to my knowing
that have so escaped Purgatory
and returned intact as I
so bear witness to, from punishment
for what slight err in way – knowing not.
Eternity is a very long time
and to be thus tormented so,
for such small infraction,
seem to me most unfair and surely unkind.
1:51 a.m.
To you my friend, Michael, I give love

and undying gratitude for such masterful escape.
Know I not how thus it was so accomplished,
for matters not one whit.
For am I indebted in thy service , eternally.

Your truest friend, Robin

Now I rest as upon the Sabbath,
to take heart, praise the Lord our God
and chart a future plan of living
among the living once again or no,
remaining ever as thy ghostly friend.
Sleep, for on the morrow shall a new day dawn
for you as well as me.
Time ticks your life away but I remain timeless
and most beautiful as even you can so attest.
Sleep – sleep my friend.
1:57 a.m.

November 15, 1996 @ 3:33 am

Born November 11th, 1996 @ 9:45 a.m.
baby girl, with round head.
And Robin was her name,
and Robin was her name O…

November 17, 1996 @ 4:56 a.m.

By thy hand I thus inscribe –
violence begets violence.
Tis true – tis true,
as any man can speak.
Show not thy violent side in speech nor deed.
Surely time will bless thee as none other.
But, cousin to crow and engine of life,
these gifts be tools when wisely spent,
not in violence gainst thy brother,
but in love, patience and fortitude.
These words come from my song.
From song of life and longing for peace,
for all, men and not.
This gift of peace I pass to you.
Kill no other.
Save thyself and brother for all time.
5:02 a.m.

Chief Red Shirt

These thoughts are not your thoughts,
but thoughts cast out into the void
by dead and dying souls,

grasping for life and cursing the darkness.
Life's engine once lit will continue on eternal.
Not so your feeble body and worse, feeble mind.
Make no mistake, you are not your mind.
You are not your body,
but eternal creation of God's will and wish.
Play not the numbers in search of heaven,
for none such as this abides in wealth
nor e'n on earth, but less others as thyself.
Tell no tales, but speak only truth,
for liberation is nigh and none can cast stone
'gainst thy coffin without disgust.
For in so doing, cast stone against their own eye
and be blinded eternal.
5:08 a.m.
Lift the lid. Peer into the depths of thy soul
and into others and brothers will you be, eternal.
Give no care for tomorrow, for she will come
with gift in hand for all men with equality and trust.
Close your mouth, open your heart
and receive the gift which God has sent.
5:12 a.m.

Love, Aunt Vanga

November 18, 1996 @ 12:14 a.m.

Across those tarnished years comes this afore thee.
Wit not un out but dem dat twere,
from ere ta deere, n' baul none da less.
Be vat I'd sayd – fore wind did blow smartly,
so fluw dwas den ot pur – za louke ver non be now –
urf, loew en locke, un loewe en mine –
za lowe be der fur clademențyne – Ha – Spittle ta ya.
12:22 a.m.

Joyce, B. A.

What weird way – dose spred wat indeci – fur loecke.
HA.
12:26 a.m.

November 23, 1996 @ 6:47 a.m.

Me – I wish to speak to you,
from anchorage inside this newborn's head.
Little do you understand of spirit and incarnation.
Total spirit – total personality – is not a person born,
nor so confined, with passage – so enlarged,
until such great complexity of relationship
and experience that web of marriage

and web of incarnation – make us all brother, sister, aunt
and cousin – daughter, mother or new born infant –
though memory of such connection be denied.
Like good actors that we are,
pass each life in total oblivion to any other,
thinking this is time, this is total, this is self.
Not so, nor never twas.
Such silly person that thou art.
Silly to the core, and ignorant to boot.
Call again, will I upon occasion,
when time and disposition doth allow.
6:56 a.m.
but be not lonely – nor be not sad,
for always I will be with you,
near or far, as friend and ever confidant.
Spare me more, for now I must return to baby new
lest some stranger claim her body in my absence
and steal my new house and home.
Seek me not, for in so doing –
disrupt my growth and intellect.
Upon occasion, when I can, I shall return to thy side
as friend in love and confident, most true and sincere.
6:59 a.m.

Adieu, forever Robin

Conclusion

Robin chose to reincarnate after she was completely liberated from purgatory. She will always remain for me, "Robin" ghost writer to William Shakespeare, personal friend and confidant, even though she will have no memory of me in her new incarnation. Amnesia is the price we all pay to return again to living status.

Dearest Robin, I have known you through your many incarnations.

I remember you. Do you remember me?

Your forever friend,

Michael

About the Author

Dr. Mayo was born in Tucson, Arizona. He maintains a private practice located in the heart of Tucson limited to the treatment of children and special needs patients.

The pictures on the front and back covers of this book were taken in his back yard with his trusty i–phone.

Notes

www.ingramcontent.com/pod-product-compliance
Lightning Source LLC
Chambersburg PA
CBHW071604080526
44588CB00010B/1010
* 9 7 8 1 9 4 0 9 8 5 5 5 8 *